New Directions for Institutional Research

John F. Ryan
EDITOR-IN-CHIEF

Gloria Crisp
ASSOCIATE EDITOR

Postgraduate Outcomes of College Students

Jerold S. Laguilles

Mary Ann Coughlin

Heather A. Kelly

Allison M. Walters

EDITORS

Number 169
Jossey-Bass
San Francisco

POSTGRADUATE OUTCOMES OF COLLEGE STUDENTS
Jerold S. Laguilles, Mary Ann Coughlin, Heather A. Kelly, Allison M. Walters (eds.)
New Directions for Institutional Research, no. 169
John F. Ryan, Editor-in-Chief
Gloria Crisp, Associate Editor

NEW DIRECTIONS FOR INSTITUTIONAL RESEARCH (ISSN 0271-0579, electronic ISSN 1536-075X) is part of The Jossey-Bass Higher and Adult Education Series and is published quarterly by Wiley Subscription Services, Inc., A Wiley Company, at Jossey-Bass, One Montgomery Street, Suite 1200, San Francisco, California 94104-4594 (publication number USPS 098-830). POSTMASTER: Send address changes to New Directions for Institutional Research, Jossey-Bass, One Montgomery Street, Suite 1200, San Francisco, California 94104-4594.

INDIVIDUAL SUBSCRIPTION RATE (in USD): $89 per year US/Can/Mex, $113 rest of world; institutional subscription rate: $341 US, $381 Can/Mex, $415 rest of world. Single copy rate: $29. Electronic only–all regions: $89 individual, $341 institutional; Print & Electronic–US: $98 individual, $410 institutional; Print & Electronic–Canada/Mexico: $98 individual, $450 institutional; Print & Electronic–Rest of World: $122 individual, $484 institutional.

EDITORIAL CORRESPONDENCE should be sent to John F. Ryan at jfryan@uvm.edu.

New Directions for Institutional Research is indexed in *Academic Search* (EBSCO), *Academic Search Elite* (EBSCO), *Academic Search Premier* (EBSCO), *CIJE: Current Index to Journals in Education* (ERIC), *Contents Pages in Education* (T&F), *EBSCO Professional Development Collection* (EBSCO), *Educational Research Abstracts Online* (T&F), *ERIC Database* (Education Resources Information Center), *Higher Education Abstracts* (Claremont Graduate University), *Multicultural Education Abstracts* (T&F), *Sociology of Education Abstracts* (T&F).

Cover design: Wiley
Cover Images: © Lava 4 images | Shutterstock

Microfilm copies of issues and chapters are available in 16mm and 35mm, as well as microfi che in 105mm, through University Microfilms, Inc., 300 North Zeeb Road, Ann Arbor, Michigan 48106-1346.

www.josseybass.com

THE ASSOCIATION FOR INSTITUTIONAL RESEARCH (AIR) is the world's largest professional association for institutional researchers. The organization provides educational resources, best practices, and professional development opportunities for more than 4,000 members. Its primary purpose is to support members in the process of collecting, analyzing, and converting data into information that supports decision making in higher education.

CONTENTS

Editors' Notes

The postgraduation outcomes of college students are being more widely used as key metrics to demonstrate institutional effectiveness to both external agencies and internal stakeholders. At the federal and state levels, the job placement rates of college graduates are being used as an accountability measure and are among the many institutional key performance indicators (KPIs). The College Scorecard released by the U.S. Department of Education in September 2015 now uses postgraduate earnings data as an outcomes measure. In addition, the employment outcomes and subsequent graduate school enrollment of recent graduates by colleges and universities are used for a variety of purposes, including marketing, recruiting, and demonstrating student success.

Institutional research offices play an integral role in these data-collection efforts. For example, institutions rely on alumni surveys to collect these data; however, an underlying challenge is obtaining an adequate amount of responses in order to report useful outcomes data. Moreover, these efforts are limited in obtaining salary or earnings information.

A goal of this issue is to focus on the first-destination outcomes (e.g., earnings, employment, and graduate/professional school enrollment) of college graduates while recognizing that other outcomes are also relevant across institutional settings. Through the use of current research, case studies, and best practices, each chapter highlights how postgraduate outcomes information is collected and used across the higher education spectrum.

In Chapter 1, Mary Ann Coughlin, Jerold Laguilles, Heather Kelly, and Allison Walters present the current status of postgraduate outcomes within the American higher education landscape. They discuss the complexity of defining first-destination outcomes along with the national debate over the need for these measures and the challenges in collecting and reporting data for these outcomes. Several national efforts to report postgraduation outcomes will be discussed, such as the U.S. Department of Education's College Scorecard, National Association of Colleges and Employers (NACE) First-Destination Outcomes Survey, Post-Collegiate Outcomes Framework and Toolkit, American Association of Colleges and Universities' (AAC&U), Liberal Education America's Promise (LEAP), and Gainful Employment.

In Chapter 2, Jerold Laguilles uses a case study approach to discuss how a private college with professional programs has a 77% knowledge rate in its collection of postgraduate data. The collection effort follows the National Association of Colleges and Employers (NACE) guidelines, involves

New Directions for Institutional Research, no. 169 © 2016 Wiley Periodicals, Inc.
Published online in Wiley Online Library (wileyonlinelibrary.com) • DOI: 10.1002/ir.20165

collaboration with several offices, and uses multiple data sources. In addition to sharing information about the collection process, Laguilles focuses on how the data are used at the institutional and program level, as well as how to interpret this type of information given the institutional context.

In Chapter 3, Heather Kelly and Allison Walters present strategies employed by a public research university to adopt the National Association of Colleges and Employers (NACE) standards, survey data elements, and administrative timeline to collect first-destination outcomes of graduating students to obtain the recommended 65% knowledge rate. This evolutionary data-collection process and efforts to improve the distribution of results are discussed, along with implications for other public research universities hoping to begin or refine a first-destination survey.

In Chapter 4, Cate Rowen presents private liberal arts colleges' aspirations to prepare students for broader postgraduation outcomes beyond the economic results most often discussed in the national conversation. Articulated by AAC&U in the LEAP initiative, the value of a liberal education emerges "through the application of knowledge, skills, and responsibilities to new settings and complex problems." Rowen explores a range of efforts to expand the discussion of the "value proposition" at private liberal arts colleges. Case studies from multiple institutions reflect on the inherent challenges of interjecting the complex values of the liberal arts into a discussion focused on the financial bottom line.

In Chapter 5, Lou Guthrie explains the complexity of the community college mission and the inherent challenges in assessing student outcomes. These colleges meet a variety of needs, including the granting of associate degrees and certificates that qualify graduates for well-paying jobs with room for advancement. Beyond postgraduation outcomes, these colleges serve students who wish to use their earned credits to transfer to another, often 4-year, institution. Guthrie discusses community colleges' measures of success, including transfer activities, along with the challenges institutional research staff face when trying to explain or illustrate these outcomes to external stakeholders, such as state funding agencies, the federal government, local taxpayers, and prospective employers.

In Chapter 6, Kristina Powers and Derek MacPherson address the importance of intercampus involvement in the reporting of gainful employment student-level data. They present the U.S. Department of Education's requirements related to Gainful Employment reporting and details on the resulting metrics. Powers and MacPherson demonstrate why building relationships within the institution are critical for effective gainful employment reporting.

Finally, in Chapter 7, David Troutman and Jessica Shedd introduce state workforce data, specifically unemployment insurance (UI) wage records, as a resource for higher education institutions and systems to move beyond self-reported survey data when examining postcollegiate outcomes. Troutman and Shedd discuss the strengths and limitations of these data for informing postgraduate outcomes and considerations for working with the data most effectively. They conclude with a presentation of methodological recommendations for calculating and reporting postgraduate earnings for various stakeholders with the use of UI wage data.

This volume presents a variety of postgraduate outcomes of college students and current issues affecting the reporting of these outcomes within the American higher education landscape. Institutional researchers should be aware of the internal and external demands for these data, the strengths and challenges of the data to which they have access, and how to best communicate these data to our students, families, governments, and the public. We hope this publication will help institutional researchers better understand these issues and assist them as they contribute to the institutional, local, state, and national discussions of postgraduate outcomes.

Jerold S. Laguilles
Mary Ann Coughlin
Heather A. Kelly
Allison M. Walters
Editors

JEROLD S. LAGUILLES is the director of institutional research at Springfield College.

MARY ANN COUGHLIN is the associate vice president for academic affairs at Springfield College.

HEATHER A. KELLY is the director of institutional research at the University of Delaware.

ALLISON M. WALTERS is the assistant director of institutional research at the University of Delaware.

NEW DIRECTIONS FOR INSTITUTIONAL RESEARCH • DOI: 10.1002/ir

1

This chapter provides a big-picture view of the postgraduate outcomes landscape. In an effort to promote understanding and to communicate the value of a higher education credential to various stakeholders, five national efforts are described, each of which provides a different perspective for defining, measuring, and collecting postgraduate outcomes.

Postgraduate Outcomes in American Higher Education

Mary Ann Coughlin, Jerold S. Laguilles, Heather A. Kelly, Allison M. Walters

Institutions of higher education are under increased scrutiny from all stakeholders to define the value of the credentials that they award. Long past are the times when the value of a degree was unquestioned. This scrutiny is widespread and is found across all sectors. Demands for accountability and transparency are heard from a variety of sources, including students and their families, state and federal legislators, and the general public. These calls for scrutiny are certainly warranted. After all, we are all concerned about the rising cost of a college education, increases in student indebtedness, and lower than desired completion rates. Thus, a fundamental question that all institutions of higher education are trying to answer is: What is the value of a higher education credential, and is the investment worth the cost? On the surface, the answer to this question seems easy to define. The simple or rudimentary answer seems to be grounded in the very visible outcomes that our graduates are seeking—preparation for or advancement within a chosen profession. Yet once one goes past the surface, the question is complex and one for which simple answers are just not adequate. After all, the value of a degree or certificate goes beyond career preparation and earnings potential. Educators seek to develop lifelong learners and strive to enhance key skills, such as critical thinking, written and oral communication, quantitative reasoning, and information literacy. Furthermore, most of our institutions hold even more lofty goals, such as preparing our graduates to be better global citizens.

In this chapter, the authors seek to provide an overview for the more in-depth discussion of some of the national efforts that are ongoing to

NEW DIRECTIONS FOR INSTITUTIONAL RESEARCH, no. 169 © 2016 Wiley Periodicals, Inc.
Published online in Wiley Online Library (wileyonlinelibrary.com) • DOI: 10.1002/ir.20166

11

create better outcome measures and to provide greater transparency and accountability. Specifically, five projects will be discussed—College Scorecard, National Association of Colleges and Employers (NACE) First-Destination Outcomes, Post-Collegiate Outcomes Framework and Toolkit, and American Association of Colleges and Universities' (AAC&U), Liberal Education America's Promise (LEAP), and Gainful Employment. Through the discussion of these efforts, we will explore the challenges and difficulties in defining, collecting, and reporting evidence of these important outcomes. The challenges and issues raised within the context of these national projects will be discussed in greater depth within each of the remaining chapters of this volume.

College Scorecard: A National Call for Transparency—Access, Cost, Value, and Accountability

A discussion of national initiatives to provide more information about the outcomes of higher education would not be complete without a discussion of the College Scorecard (U.S. Department of Education, 2015a). In the fall of 2015, the Department of Education launched the first release of tools and data from the College Scorecard project. This project has provided more data than ever before to help students and families compare college costs and outcomes. The goal of the project is to provide this information to prospective students and their families, as they weigh the benefits of and costs associated with the selection of different colleges and universities. The goal was more than just providing more information, and also allows these key stakeholders to account for their own needs and educational goals. The data provided are reported by institutions as part of their federally mandated Integrated Postsecondary Education Data System (IPEDS) reporting, data on federal financial aid from Federal Student Aid office, and tax information from the Department of the Treasury. Thus, these data provide insights into the performance of schools that receive federal financial aid dollars and the outcomes of the students from those schools.

The project includes a redesigned consumer tool, as well as a data page designed specifically for researchers and policy makers. The Web-based tool was released in fall of 2015 and provides access to only a limited amount of data that were collected as part of this initiative. However, this consumer tool allows prospective students and their advocates to search for and compare options according to their specifications. The results presented allow comparison of institutions based upon measures of access, affordability, and outcomes. As a result of the release of this tool, comparisons can now be made of students' earnings after attending an institution, the percentage of students who earn more than the average high school graduate, the cumulative debt of students, and loan repayment rates for borrowers. Other consumer information, such as the available areas of study, the rate at which first-year students choose to return the following year, and details about the particular mission of the school (e.g., minority-serving institutions) is also presented for each institution in the Web-based tool.

As described in the technical paper on the Scorecard (U.S. Department of Education, 2015b), the data behind the Scorecard include a vast array of data on student completion, debt and repayment, and earnings. The data are disaggregated by various student subgroups, which include first-generation students and low-income students, as well as federal Pell Grant recipients. The entire data set spans nearly 20 years of information from more than 7,000 institutions. The compilation of these data is a result of collaboration across multiple federal agencies. The data set includes elements from the Integrated Postsecondary Education Data System (IPEDS), the National Student Loan Data System (NSLDS), and administrative earnings data from tax records maintained by the Department of the Treasury. What makes the public release of this data set even more useful is that the Department of Education released the data through an open application program interface (API). The API provides greater ease in the transfer and update of this data and allows the development of new applications and tools by outside organizations. By the end of the 2015 calendar year, the Department had identified over 15 organizations that are already using and building on the data to conduct their own analyses, and were releasing the data on their own Web sites and through their own mobile tools.

Even though the release of the College Scorecard represents a significant step forward in the data that are nationally available on college costs and outcomes, it is not without its limitations. A technical review panel was held in December of 2015 and noted multiple data limitations (RTI International, 2014). A few important data limitations include: the classification of institutions, which impacts what institutions are included in the College Scorecard; branch campuses and the level of aggregation that is used when data files are merged across federal sources; and the use of earnings data to represent labor-market outcomes.

For the College Scorecard, institutions are classified by predominant award level, based on the number and level of awards that the institutions reported on the IPEDS Completions component. This classification places limitations on the initial release of the Scorecard data and tools in two ways. First, institutions that predominantly award certificates were excluded from the first release of the consumer tool, although their data do appear in the full data file. This omission primarily affected community colleges and other 2-year degree-granting institutions that awarded more certificates than degrees. It is important to note that many of these institutions serve and are closely connected to the student populations in their areas, offering affordable options for these students. Thus, not including these institutions in the Web-based tool limits information and options for prospective students and their advisors. The classification of institutions by predominant degree also creates limitations through the classification of institutions by the highest educational offering. For example, a community college that awards more associate's degrees than bachelor's degrees in a given year is classified as a predominantly associate's degree-granting institution and labeled a 2-year (associate's) school on the consumer tool. Yet although the institution does offer bachelor's program, it is not included in the search results for 4-year institutions. Thus, the 2-year label could lead prospective students seeking bachelor's degrees to assume that these regional colleges that offer degrees across multiple award levels do not meet their needs.

As described above, many institutions of higher education are complex and are positioned to offer instruction in a variety of different ways (RTI International, 2014). In addition, many institutions are often comprised of multiple different campus, branches, or instructional locations. Currently, different federal agencies have different reporting requirements for reporting data for the different campus entities. Also, different agencies use different institutional identifiers for the various campus locations. Thus, the combination of data from different sources limits how data can be presented for institutions with branch campuses. Within the Scorecard, when institutions with multiple campuses manage and administer financial aid for all branches of the institution through the main campus, the student debt and earnings data are rolled up to the main campus level and the data listed for the branch campuses are duplicated for all of the campus entities. On the surface, treating the data in this manner appears to be quite logical; however, offerings and outcomes at branch campuses may vary greatly. For example, one institution may offer only bachelor's degree programs at the main campus and offer a smaller associate degree program at a branch campus. Because the institution reports both campuses under separate IPEDS ids and reports financial aid through the main campus, their student debt and earnings data are aggregated to the main campus level and duplicated for the branch campus in Scorecard. Therefore, potential exists that prospective students would conclude that graduates of the 2-year program at the regional campus would have the same earnings as 4-year degree graduates from the main campus. In addition, the reported earnings do not accurately represent either program because of the aggregation across both of these programs. Although this data limitation does have a large impact for some institutions, it is important to note that many institutions have only one main campus and are reported consistently across the different federal agencies.

Earnings are used as the proxy measure for the labor-market outcomes within the Scorecard (RTI International, 2014). To produce earnings for each institution in the Scorecard, the cohort of federally aided students for the institution are identified. Next, the earnings data for individuals in the cohort are aggregated together from deidentified tax records. Thus, the earnings data apply to entry cohort of federally aided students and unfortunately the measure does not account for completion status, as both graduates and nongraduates are included in the initial cohort. In addition, outcomes for students may vary as much within the same institution based on student subgroups and program of study as these data do across an institution. So clearly, prospective students cannot conclude causality from these data and ideally these data need to be disaggregated at the program level. Although the College Scorecard does represent an advancement in national data on access, cost, and accountability of higher education institutions, more work is needed. This work not only includes addressing the data limitations, but it also will require more complete and detailed information about the post-collegiate outcomes of graduates at the institution and discipline level.

NACE—First-Destination Outcomes

The National Association of Colleges and Employers (NACE) is a professional association of college career services, university relations, and recruiting professionals. NACE has a distinctive mission to "lead the community of professionals focused on the employment of the college educated by providing access to relevant knowledge, resources, insight, and relationship" (National Association of Colleges and Employers [NACE], 2014, p. 1). NACE has long advocated for institutions to compile and report the postgraduation outcomes of their students. Specifically, NACE has called for colleges and universities to collect and report on a comprehensive set of first-destination outcomes of college graduates. NACE advocated for the need for more than just employment outcomes, also stressing the importance of continuing education and public and private service results. In addition, although many institutions of higher education regularly report such outcomes, relatively few efforts exist that follow consistent protocols in the collection and reporting of these data. A need exists for reporting entities to use common definitions for outcomes, apply consistent methods for data collection, and follow a uniform time frame for collecting and reporting data. After all, without following these basic tenets of research methodology, how can the data be appropriately used for consumer and public policy information?

In January 2014, NACE published initial standards and guidelines that were intended to assess outcomes for students graduating with either an associate's or bachelor's degree immediately after their undergraduate experience—first-destination outcomes (NACE, 2014). This distinction is important to note, as measuring the long-term career prospects of these graduates presents a whole other set of methodological challenges. Another important element defined by these guidelines is the consistent definition of a knowledge rate. Knowledge rate is defined as "the percent of graduates for which the institution has reasonable and verifiable information concerning the graduates' postgraduation career activities" (NACE, 2014, p. 6). Reasonable and verifiable information can come from many sources—surveys, social media (LinkedIn), parents, faculty, and employers. Of course, the key in this definition is that the information should also be verifiable and the standards call for institutions to "make good faith efforts to verify the information obtained by any source other than the graduate or in any case where there is some concern about the accuracy of the available information" (NACE, 2014, p. 6). Collecting these data from recent graduates can be difficult and often studies suffer from poor response rates and fall woefully short in providing an accurate representation of the entire cohort of students. These guidelines call for institutions to have the highest possible rate, and encourage institutions to reach a minimum knowledge rate of 65%.

A segment of the NACE college membership adopted the standards as guidelines for collecting the results on their individual campuses, and in January 2015, NACE called upon its membership to share their results for the Class of 2014. In total, data from over 200 institutions reported on the graduating classes from these institutions. The data shared represented nearly 274,000 graduates at both the bachelor's and associate's level (NACE, 2015). The release of these data was touted to be another first in producing credible measures of the outcome of higher education. Some key findings at the national level included the fact that:

> Of associate degree graduates, 20 percent of the group was going on to continue their education. (NACE, 2015, p. 9)

> Of the bachelor's degree recipients, just over 16 percent of the group reporting continuing their education. (NACE, 2015, p. 12)

> Just over 80 percent of bachelor's degree graduates reported a positive outcome, (i.e., employment, self-employment, service/military, or continuing education) within the six-month period following graduation. The percentage is even higher for those graduating with an associate degree—85 percent. (NACE, 2015, p. 11)

Although the efforts of NACE represent another step forward to collect these data consistently, the effort is not without its limitations. First, the NACE sample, although of decent size, does not represent a true national sample. The sample represented a voluntary effort and is overrepresentative of institutions from the public and private not-for-profit sectors (NACE, 2015). In fact, only one private for-profit institution participated in the initial study. Further, as would be expected, the variation in career outcomes across the academic disciplines of the graduates was as varied as the career outcomes between different types of institutions. Thus, although data in the initial report are broken out by 31 academic disciplines, the sample size within disciplines and across sectors severely limits the generalizability of these results. Within this volume, multiple chapter authors will report and describe their experiences in working with these NACE guidelines and will further illuminate both the strengths and challenges associated with this protocol.

Postcollegiate Outcome Framework and Toolkit

The American Association of Community Colleges (AACC) led a post-collegiate outcomes initiative (PCO) in collaboration with two partner organizations—Association of Public and Land-grant Universities (APLU) and the American Association of State Colleges and Universities (AASCU). The initiative was developed to broaden the conversation surrounding post-collegiate outcomes and was funded by the Bill and Melinda Gates Foundation. The initiative was specifically focused on providing a framework to expand these important discussions surrounding the outcomes and value of higher education (The American Association of Community Colleges, American Association of State Colleges and Universities, and the Association of Public and Land-grant Universities [AACC, AASCU, and APLU], 2015a). A major premise of the initiative is that these outcomes should include both economic and social contributions of graduates. Also, the framework sought to define metrics that could be used to measure these contributions to both individuals and their communities [AACC, AASCU, and APLU] (2015b).

The framework as defined by working groups that consisted of subject matter experts and national leaders from both 2- and 4-year public institutions consist of two intersecting intersection of two dimensions—public/personal and economic/human capital. It is important to note that both dimensions fall on underlying continuum. Thus, when both are presented on a continuum the resulting framework consists of a grid with four quadrants formed by the intersection of two dimensions.

The overview of the PCO framework defines these four quadrants as follows, which can be seen in Figure 1.1.

The intersection of public and economic in the top left quadrant includes outcomes related to the public economic good. The intersection of public and human capital in the bottom left quadrant represents outcomes related to the public social or civic capital value of higher education. The intersection of the personal and economic in the top right quadrant encompasses outcomes related to the personal (or individual) economic good. And the intersection of personal and human capital in the bottom right quadrant indicates outcomes that demonstrate the personal (or individual) capital value. (AACC, AASCU, and APLU, 1998, p. 8).

The simplicity of this model was grounded in the work of the Institute for Higher Education Policy (IHEP, 2014), who also developed a structure for classifying the benefits of higher education, as mentioned by AACC, AASCU, and APLU (2015c) in the PCO framework development. Thus, the next step in the development of this PCO framework was necessary to forward and distinguish this work beyond that of others. That next step was the development of a framework for consistent and meaningful measurement tools. As a result, parts of the Framework Toolkit provide an in-depth discussion of key elements of collecting and measuring these important

NEW DIRECTIONS FOR INSTITUTIONAL RESEARCH • DOI: 10.1002/ir

Figure 1.1. PCO Conceptual Framework

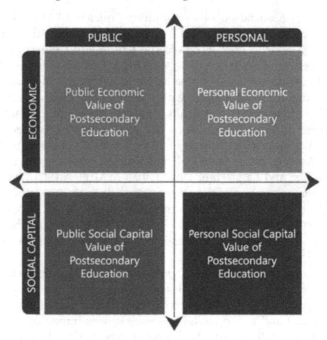

outcomes, such as: intended audience, time frame, level of analysis, and intentionality. Another part of the framework discusses the important distinction between outcomes, metrics, and indicators. Certainly, this theoretical framework and practical toolkit is a valuable resource to the higher education community. Within this volume, multiple chapter authors will report and describe their efforts and the challenges involved with reporting outcomes that go beyond the immediate economic value of a college education.

Liberal Education and America's Promise

In 1998, the board of the American Association of Colleges and Universities (AAC&U) endorsed a statement on liberal education. The statement defines liberal education as "one that prepares us to live responsible, productive, and creative lives in a dramatically changing world. It is an education that fosters a well-grounded intellectual resilience, a disposition toward lifelong learning, and an acceptance of responsibility for the ethical consequences of our ideas and actions" (American Association of Colleges and Universities [AAC&U], 1998, para. 1). This definition of liberal education underscores the complexity of trying to answer the fundamental question: What is the value of a higher education credential and is the investment worth the cost?

So, how do institutions of higher education provide evidence that we have prepared our graduates to live responsible and productive lives in a dramatically changing world?

The Liberal Education and America's Promise (LEAP) initiative, which was undertaken in 2005 by AAC&U, provides a framework for this discussion. LEAP is a broad-based initiative that includes advocacy for the principles of liberal education, support for campus action that enhances student learning and student engagement, as well as research to enhance our knowledge of liberal education and document student achievement of these essential learning outcome. This last goal of the initiative to "document national, state, and institutional progress in student achievement of Essential Learning Outcomes" provides the basis and guidance by which Institutional Researchers can help to answer these larger more complex questions about the value of higher education (AAC&U, 2005, p. 1).

Four broad essential learning outcomes are promoted by LEAP. They include Knowledge of Human Cultures and the Physical and Natural World, Intellectual and Practical Skills, Personal and Social Responsibility, and Integrative and Applied Learning. Each of these outcomes cannot be achieved simply through participation in a general education curriculum or any one course of study rather they call for an intentional and integrated curriculum. Through study in the sciences and mathematics, social sciences, humanities, histories, languages, and the arts, Knowledge of Human Cultures and the Physical and Natural World focuses on engagement with the larger overarching questions that are enduring and/or contemporary (AAC&U, 2005, p. 4). Intellectual and Practical Skills are skills that employers have recognized as more important for their employees to possess than the specific skills of any one major (AAC&U, 2013). These skills include inquiry and analysis, critical and creative thinking, written and oral communication, quantitative literacy, information literacy, and teamwork and problem solving. The LEAP framework calls for these skills to be thoroughly integrated across the curriculum and presented to students in a series of progressively more complex and challenging problems and projects (AAC&U, 2005)

The next essential learning outcome, Personal and Social Responsibility, stresses the importance of active student involvement with diverse cultures and experiences that provide real-world challenges to students. The Personal and Social Responsibility learning outcome focuses on civic knowledge and engagement at both the local and global level, emphasizes intercultural knowledge and competence, promotes ethical reasoning and action, and instills the foundation and skills for lifelong learning (AAC&U, 2005). When surveyed employers also reported that "colleges and universities should also place more emphasis on helping students develop the ability to apply knowledge and skills to real-world settings through internships or other hands-on experiences" (AAC&U, 2013, p. 12). The last of the essential learning outcomes, Integrative and Applied Learning, emphasizes that learning needs to be applied in these real-world settings. Thus, this

NEW DIRECTIONS FOR INSTITUTIONAL RESEARCH • DOI: 10.1002/ir

outcome stresses that students need to demonstrate their learning "through the application of knowledge, skills, and responsibilities to new settings and complex problems" (AAC&U, 2005, p. 4).

Certainly, these essential learning outcomes define the framework for answering the more complex and nuanced questions regarding the value of our higher education credentials. But providing evidence that we are in fact achieving these outcomes is not achieved by defining the outcomes. To extend the framework, the LEAP initiative promotes participation in High-Impact Practices (HIP). These practices are positively associated with student learning and retention, as they facilitate learning outside of the classroom, require meaningful interactions with faculty and students, and provide frequent and substantive feedback to students. These practices include: first-year seminars and experiences, common intellectual experiences, learning communities, writing-intensive courses, collaborative assignments and projects, undergraduate research, diversity and global learning, service learning and community-based learning, internships, and capstone courses and projects (Kuh, 2008). Documentation of student participation in these activities is certainly a fundamental form of evidence. Yet, documentation of student experiences or even student perception of the value of these experiences as provided by instruments, such as the National Survey of Student Engagement (NSSE), does not provide evidence of the extent to which our graduates have acquired the skills defined in the essential learning outcomes. Thus, the LEAP initiative promotes the use of authentic assessment in providing a more direct assessment of the extent to which our graduates have achieved these essential learning outcomes.

The Valid Assessment of Learning in Undergraduate Education (VALUE) project has provided rubrics that can be applied to the authentic assessment of student learning. As part of this project, AAC&U brought together teams of faculty and other educational professionals from institutions from all sectors, institutional types, and geographic regions. The teams developed rubrics for 16 elements associated with the Essential Learning Outcomes. Each VALUE rubric contains the most common and broadly shared criteria or core characteristics considered relevant for judging the quality of student work in each of the outcome areas. The VALUE rubrics reflect faculty expectations for the essential learning outcomes regardless of type of institution, mission, size, or location. Also, these VALUE rubrics are structured to demonstrate, share, and assess student accomplishment of progressively more advanced levels of student learning that span the development of these skills (AAC&U, 2009). The use of rubrics for the authentic assessment of student learning can present many logistical issues both in terms of the collection of student work and the appropriate training of qualified evaluators. However, a recent multistate collaboration between AAC&U and State Higher Education Executive Officers (SHEEO) Association has provided evidence that that rubric-based assessment can be taken to scale and can produce valid findings with credible and actionable information about student learning across multiple different institutions (SHEEO, 2015).

Gainful Employment

It truly is hard to classify the U.S. Department of Education Gainful Employment rule as a new initiative; after all it has been in existence since 2011. Given the turbulent history of the regulations and the fact that data were not reported until July 31, 2015, it certainly has been the focus of many recently as an initiative designed to provide metrics on postgraduation outcomes. Thus as we close this chapter, we wanted to provide some context and background on gainful employment.

So you might ask, what is the current state of the Gainful Employment regulations? Well as of early March 2016, a federal appeals court upheld a lower court ruling which rejected claims by the Association of Private Sector Colleges and Universities that the rule's metrics were arbitrary and lacked congressional authority. The appeals court affirmed that the Department of Education had the right, if not the responsibility to define gainful employment with debt to earning ratios.

The court stated "it would be strange for Congress to loan out money to train students for jobs that were insufficiently remunerative to permit the students to repay their loans" and summarized that "had Congress been uninterested in whether the loan-funded training would result in a job that paid enough to satisfy loan debt, it would have created a federal grant system instead of a federal loan system focusing on preparation for gainful employment" (Appeal from the U.S. District Court for the District of Columbia, 2016, p. 3). Thus as of the writing of this volume, gainful employment regulations are in existence. These regulations, while originally were written to target for-profit institutions, impact all institutions of higher education that provide programs utilizing federal funding to support students enrolled in postsecondary degree and certificate programs. Although it is clear that all for-profit institutions are subject to gainful employment regulations for all but a few programs, all other institutions are also subject to gainful employment regulation for any certificate programs that are offered at either the undergraduate or graduate level for which students are receiving federal financial aid.

So where are we now? The Federal Registry (Federal Registry, 2011) documents the Department of Education's Program Integrity: Gainful Employment–Debt Measures rule. The regulations recognize that many institutions provide gainful employment programs that offer important opportunities for students to expand their skills while earning postsecondary degrees and certificates. Although recognizing that many quality programs exist, the regulations are particularly focused on identifying those programs that "leave large numbers of students with unaffordable debts and poor employment prospects" (Federal Registry, 2011, p. 8). Thus, the gainful employment regulations are designed to:

> provide institutions with better metrics and more time to assess their program outcomes and thereby a greater opportunity to improve the performance of their gainful employment programs before those programs lose eligibility for Federal student aid funds, and (2) identify accurately the worst performing gainful employment programs. At the same time, the final regulations require that these federally funded programs meet minimal standards because students and taxpayers have too much at stake to allow otherwise. (Federal Registry, 2011, p. 9).

These regulations are still heavily debated and criticized. Key constituent groups take opposite points of view. Some feel that the regulations are too restrictive and will deny federal financial assistance to students seeking postsecondary education credentials; others feel that the regulations do not go far enough to regulate the use of federal funds for students in these programs. Nonetheless, these regulations are in fact reporting requirements for all institutions receiving title IV funding for these programs. Thus, institutions are currently working to develop appropriate systems for accurately complying with these regulations. In Chapter 6, Powers and MacPherson provide greater details about these regulations and background for leading gainful employment metric reporting.

References

American Association of Colleges and Universities. (1998). Statement on liberal learning. https://www.aacu.org/about/statements/liberal-learning
American Association of Colleges and Universities. (2005). Introduction to leap. Pp. 1–8. https://www.aacu.org/sites/default/files/files/LEAP/Introduction_to_LEAP.pdf
American Association of Colleges and Universities. (2009). Value. https://www.aacu.org/value
American Association of Colleges and Universities. (2013). It takes more than a major. Pp. 1–15. https://www.aacu.org/leap/presidentstrust/compact/2013SurveySummary
The American Association of Community Colleges, American Association of State Colleges and Universities, and Association of Public and Land-Grant Universities. (2015a). Background. http://www.aacc.nche.edu/AboutCC/Trends/pco/Pages/background
The American Association of Community Colleges, American Association of State Colleges and Universities, and Association of Public and Land-Grant Universities. (2015b). Dimensions to consider when creating post-collegiate outcomes measure. Pp. 1–7. http://www.aacc.nche.edu/AboutCC/Trends/pco/Documents/PCO_Dimensions.pdf
The American Association of Community Colleges, American Association of State Colleges and Universities, and Association of Public and Land-Grant Universities. (2015c). Post-collegiate outcomes initiatives: Overview. Pp. 1–8. http://www.aacc.nche.edu/AboutCC/Trends/pco/Documents/PCO_Overview.pdf

NEW DIRECTIONS FOR INSTITUTIONAL RESEARCH • DOI: 10.1002/ir

Appeal from the United States District Court for the District of Columbia. (2016). United States Court of Appeals FOR THE DISTRICT OF COLUMBIA CIRCUIT. ASSOCIATION OF PRIVATE SECTOR COLLEGES AND UNIVERSITIES, APPELLANT v. ARNE DUNCAN, IN HIS OFFICIAL CAPACITY AS SECRETARY OF THE DEPARTMENT OF EDUCATION, OFFICE OF THE SECRETARY, ET AL., APPELLEES. FILED ON: MARCH 8, 2016. Pp. 1–4. https://www.documentcloud.org /documents/2753140-DC-Circuit-Court-of-Appeals-Court-Rejects-For.html

Federal Registry. (2011). DEPARTMENT OF EDUCATION 34 CFR Part 668. Rules and Regulations. 76. https://www.federalregister.gov/articles/2011/06/13/2011-13905 /program-integrity-gainful-employment-debt-measures

Institute for Higher Education Policy. (1998). *Reaping the benefits: Defining the public and private value of going to college.* Washington, DC: Institute for Higher Education Policy.

Kuh, G. D. (2008). *High-impact educational practices: What they are, who has access to them and why they matter.* Washington, DC: Association of American College and Universities.

National Association of Colleges and Employers. (2014). National Association of Colleges and Employers. 2014–17. Strategic Plan. Pp. 1–4. http://www.naceweb.org /uploadedFiles/Content/static-assets/downloads/nace-strategic-plan.pdf

National Association of Colleges and Employers. (2015). The NACE first-destination survey. http://www.naceweb.org/surveys/first-destination.aspx

RTI International. (2014). College Scorecard Technical Review Panel. Report and suggestions from College Scorecard technical review panel 1: # information. Pp. 1–8. https://edsurveys.rti.org/cs_trp/index.aspx

State Higher Education Executive Officers (SHEEO) Association. (2015). MSC: A multi-state collaborative to advance learning outcomes assessment. http://www.sheeo .org/msc

U.S. Department of Education. (2015a). College Scorecard Data. Better information for better college choice & institutional performance. Pp. 1–29. https://collegescorecard. ed.gov/assets/BetterInformationForBetterCollegeChoiceAndInstitutionalPerformance .pdf

U.S. Department of Education. (2015b). College Scorecard Data. Using federal data to measure and improve the performance of U.S. institutions of higher education. Pp. 1–84. https://collegescorecard.ed.gov/assets/UsingFederalDataToMeasureAndImp rovePerformance.pdf

MARY ANN COUGHLIN *is the associate vice president for academic affairs at Springfield College.*

JEROLD S. LAGUILLES *is the director of institutional research at Springfield College.*

HEATHER A. KELLY *is the director of institutional research at the University of Delaware.*

ALLISON M. WALTERS *is the assistant director of institutional research at the University of Delaware.*

NEW DIRECTIONS FOR INSTITUTIONAL RESEARCH • DOI: 10.1002/ir

2

This chapter describes the background and process for collecting postgraduation outcomes data at a 4-year not-for-profit private college. The strategies, analyses, and reporting of this data-collection effort are highlighted with the use of a case study.

Collecting and Using Postgraduate Outcomes Data at a Private College

Jerold S. Laguilles

In response to the external pressures from federal policy makers, state law-makers, families, and students about the value of a postsecondary education, colleges and universities typically report on the career outcomes of their recent graduates. Collecting these data is not a new endeavor but in the absence of any guiding standards, it is not uncommon for institutions to use different collection methods and reporting methods, which ultimately limits the ability to compare data and the usefulness of said data (Rogers, 2013). To address this issue, the National Association of Colleges and Employers (NACE) released guidelines for the collection and reporting of outcomes data for new college graduates in 2014 (NACE, 2014). As of this writing, the standards and protocols for college postgraduate outcomes data are still fairly new, having just completed their inaugural year. However, as more institutions participate in sharing their outcomes data with NACE, institutional research offices are central to this collection effort along with their colleagues in career services, and should be aware of both the benefits and challenges related to these data.

This chapter will use an institutional case study approach, and discuss how the institutional research office at Springfield College (Massachusetts) has helped to implement the NACE guidelines successfully over the past few years, how the results of this data collection have been used, and what challenges remain. Over a period of 5 years, the data-collection process evolved from being the responsibility of a single office to its current state as a multi-office collaboration coordinated by institutional research. In the most recent data collection, a 77% knowledge rate and a 96% career outcomes rate were achieved for bachelor-degree recipients. In many ways, the postgraduate outcomes data collection at this institution is the most resource-intensive effort, but arguably one of the most important projects conducted each academic year.

NEW DIRECTIONS FOR INSTITUTIONAL RESEARCH, no. 169 © 2016 Wiley Periodicals, Inc.
Published online in Wiley Online Library (wileyonlinelibrary.com) • DOI: 10.1002/ir.20167

Institutional Background and Initial Challenges

As a private, not-for-profit college, the Basic Carnegie Classification of Springfield College is Master's Colleges & Universities: Larger Programs (The Carnegie Classification of Institutions of Higher Education, n.d.). The mission statement of the College is to "educate students in spirit, mind, and body for leadership in service to others." In support of this mission, the College prepares students with real-world leadership skills for careers that transform lives and communities and offers a range of undergraduate and graduate degree programs in the fields of health sciences, human and social services, sport management and movement studies, education, business, and the arts and sciences. It also offers doctoral programs in physical education, physical therapy, and counseling psychology. Several programs in the health sciences have dual-degree programs options (5- or 6-year program lengths) in which students earn a bachelor's of science degree in 4 years on their way toward completing a master's or doctoral degree.

Similar to institutions with comparable characteristics, the employment outcomes of recent graduates, especially in professional majors, is an important measure of institutional success. Prior responsibility for collecting and reporting these data resided with the career services office. However, poor data quality plagued the early data-collection efforts, most notably with low survey response rates (approximately 30%) and inconsistent survey administrations, as the data were collected during the busy commencement weekend and via e-mail follow-up after graduation. These challenges also hindered the reporting of these outcomes, as key stakeholders, such as vice presidents, academic deans, and department chairs, sought the breakout of postgraduation outcomes at the school, department, and program levels. At the same time, prospective students and their families were also interested in the types of employment opportunities available to recent graduates of specific majors. The desire for this information is understandable, given that nearly 70% of college seniors graduate with student loan debt (The Institute for College Access and Success, 2014).

It was under these circumstances that the primary responsibility for collecting postgraduate outcomes data for recent graduates moved to the institutional research office. Over a 2-year period, institutional research created a survey instrument, administered the survey, analyzed the results, and prepared reports. The data collection became more standardized and consistent, and the mixed-mode administration of using a Web-based survey along with telephone follow-up calling yielded response rates in the 40–45% range. Despite being an improvement, this response rate was still not large enough to report results at the department or program level. In addition, item nonresponse resulted in poor data quality for questions pertaining to current salary. Furthermore, a need for career-outcomes data from advanced degree programs was also increasing, and the response rates for graduates from graduate programs were even lower than for bachelor-degree recipients.

A Collaborative Effort

Several years ago, the institutional research office forged a new partnership with the newly hired director of career services to improve the postgraduation-outcomes data collection. From an institutional research perspective, the most important aspects were to maintain a systematic data-collection process with an acceptable response rate. From the career services side, the desire to report on positive employment and/or subsequent graduate school enrollment outcomes to internal and external audiences was strong. The key linchpin, however, was receiving an adequate number of responses from a population of individuals (i.e., recent graduates) for which the institution has unreliable contact information. Both offices also recognized that additional campus stakeholders should be involved in this process, and representatives from the offices of enrollment management and communications as well as academic deans were invited to collaborate on this project. Enrollment management regularly fields questions from prospective students and parents about the career outcomes of specific majors, the office of communications reports these data publicly to promote the institution, and academic deans share this information with departments for program review and accreditation purposes. Having multiple offices invested in this effort not only clarified the purpose of this data-collection process, but also signaled the institutional importance of reporting on our graduates' immediate college outcomes.

NACE First-Destination Survey Standards and Protocols

In 2014, because of the growing interest by various stakeholders outside and within higher education, NACE developed standards and protocols for colleges and universities to use in collecting and reporting career outcomes data of graduating students. According to NACE, the standards and protocols were "designed to address the growing demand by accrediting bodies and governmental agencies for more consistent, comparable, and reliable outcomes data" (NACE, 2014). In addition, NACE provided the opportunity for individual institutions to share their outcomes data as a way to track national trends and to provide comparison data. The NACE protocols provided useful guidelines in the following areas: defining the graduating class, the use of knowledge rates versus response rates, and providing guidance on career outcomes reporting statuses.

Defining the Graduating Class Population.   In previous data collections at Springfield College, the graduating class was simply the spring (May) graduates of the academic year. Subsequent data collections expanded this population to include summer (August) graduates. The NACE standards recommended that institutions follow the reporting requirements established by the National Center for Education Statistics' Integrated Postsecondary Education Data System (IPEDS) program for degree completions in which each year's graduating class includes those students who completed degrees between the periods of July 1 to June 30 each year. For example, the Class of 2014 for this institution would comprise of graduates between July 1, 2013 and June 30, 2014 and include graduates from three conferral periods: August, December, and May.

Knowledge Rates.   Traditionally, colleges and universities administer surveys to recent alumni asking about their current career activities and calculate a response rate based on the number of alumni who respond to the survey out of the population surveyed. At Springfield College, the typical response rate was around 40%. In lieu of response rates, NACE advocates the use of a knowledge rate, which is defined as "the percent of graduates for which the institution has reasonable and verifiable information concerning the graduates' post-graduation career activities" (NACE, 2014). In addition to self-reported data from graduates, other verifiable data sources may be used to collect this information, including employers, faculty, parents, and on-line sources, such as LinkedIn. In other words, do institutions "know" if their graduates are currently employed, enrolled in graduate or professional school, in the military, in volunteer service, currently unemployed, etc.? With the use of this approach, the knowledge rate is a bit broader and more flexible in discerning current statuses, because it is not simply limited to whether a person responded to a survey or not. Finally, NACE suggests that institutions strive for a knowledge rate of at least 65% for baccalaureate degree-seeking students.

Career Outcomes Rate.   NACE also provide guidance on the reporting of the career outcomes of an institution's graduates. Typically, colleges and universities report the job placement rates of their recent graduates, but this rate tends to overemphasize employment outcomes. A more complete picture of an institution's outcomes should also represent the proportion of recent graduates in other possible postgraduate settings, including continuing education or volunteer service. The career outcomes rate is defined as the percentage of graduates in the following categories: employed full-time, employed part-time, participating in a program of voluntary service, serving in the U.S. Armed Forces, or enrolled in a program of continuing education out of all graduates with a known status (NACE, 2014). The use of this rate encompasses and acknowledges that graduates could be in a number of positive career outcomes.

New Institutional Effort

After becoming more familiar with the NACE First-Destination Standards and Protocols, institutional research and the career center agreed to follow the new protocols and set a goal to achieve a 65% response rate or higher. In addition, upon consulting with the relevant campus stakeholders, there were also internal goals to report the institution's data at the academic school and program level and to create a publication piece of this information to be shared with external audiences.

Data Sources.   In order to achieve the minimum 65% knowledge rate, five distinct data sources were identified and used to determine the postgraduate status of the graduating class. Each year, approximately 25–30% of the bachelor-degree recipients continue their education in a graduate program at Springfield College, with a majority of these students completing a dual-degree program in the health sciences. Thus, the first data source consists of using institutional enrollment records to identify these students and to categorize their status as continuing their education. The second data source is the self-reported information from recent graduates using the traditional methods of an online survey administered view e-mail and telephone follow-up calls. The third data source consisted of determining which undergraduate degree recipients subsequently enroll in a graduate program at another institution. Subsequent enrollment was identified by using the StudentTracker service of the National Student Clearinghouse (NSC), which provides continuing collegiate enrollment and degree information on current and former students as well as former admission applicants. The fourth data source used information from the LinkedIn profiles of the recent graduates. Lastly, faculty members were asked to provide any career outcomes information to round out the data collection.

It is worth noting that at the very minimum each of these data sources will provide career status information that is used to determine the institutional knowledge rates and career outcomes rate. However, the data sources differ in the amount of other postgraduate information that is provided to the institution. For example, graduates who respond to the online or telephone survey have the opportunity to share much more information about their current career status including full or part-time status, employer name, job title, salary, employment location, etc. The institutional graduate enrollment records and NSC StudentTracker information provide solid information on which graduates continue their education, including full- or part-time enrollment, graduate program name, and graduate institution. Finally, the data obtained from faculty and LinkedIn provide the least amount of career-outcomes data other than current status of the recent graduates. Figure 2.1 summarizes this hierarchical nature of these five data sources.

Data-Collection Administration

To illustrate how Springfield College was able to improve a 30% response rate to a 77% knowledge rate for bachelor's degree recipients in its most recent collection of postgraduate outcomes data, the following section will provide details on various aspects of the data-collection process.

New Directions for Institutional Research • DOI: 10.1002/ir

Figure 2.1. Postgraduate Outcomes Data Sources

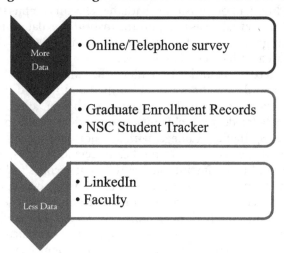

Population.   The most recent graduating class (2014–2015) for this data collection included degree recipients from three conferral periods: August 2014, December 2014, and May 2015. As noted in the NACE protocols, these conferral periods are consistent with the IPEDS completions reporting period. A total of 955 individuals were awarded degrees in this graduating class with 525 bachelor-degree recipients and 430 graduate degree recipients. In preparation for survey administration, academic program information was generated for each member of the graduating class from the institutional database. This information included data fields, such as academic major, academic department, school, degree earned, and degree date. In addition, personal contact information, including name, e-mail address, and phone number were also generated and used for the survey administration.

Instrument.   The instrument used to collect the postgraduate outcomes data was informed by the NACE guidelines. Specifically, the question asking about the primary status of the recent graduates followed the format provided by the NACE sample survey. The response choices for this question included employed full-time, employed part-time, participating in a volunteer or service program, serving in the U.S. military, enrolled in a program of continuing education, seeking employment, planning to continue education but not yet enrolled, not seeking employment, or continuing education at this time (NACE, 2014). This is the single most important data item of this data collection because the responses to this question determine not only the knowledge rate but also the career outcomes rate. Other survey items include additional questions asking about employer names, job titles, salary, location graduation school institution, graduate school program, and degree level. Institutional research designed the instrument in Qualtrics, a survey software provider, and optimized the survey for Web administration by including authentication, skip logic, personalized e-mail invitation messages, and automatic reminders to nonrespondents.

Timeline.   The data-collection period for the 2014–2015 graduating classes spanned 3 months from October 1 to December 31, 2015. There were six distinct steps in data-collection process. First, members of the graduating class who subsequently enrolled in a graduate or professional program, were temporarily removed from the survey population because their statuses as continuing their education are known from institutional enrollment records. Second, the Web survey was administered to the remaining members of the graduating class via e-mail during the first week of October 2015. Over the next 3 weeks, three follow-up e-mails were also sent to nonresponders, reminding the recent graduates to participate in the survey. Current and reliable e-mail addresses can be difficult to obtain for this population, so the third step involved a telephone administration of the postgraduate outcomes survey to all individuals who did not respond to the Web survey. The telephone-calling effort took place in the first week of November 2015. In the fourth step, the names of remaining nonrespondents from the Web and telephone administration efforts were sent to the NSC Student Tracker service in mid-November 2015 to determine whether any individuals subsequently enrolled in a continuing education program at another institution. In the fifth step, the career center used LinkedIn to determine the current career outcomes of the remaining individuals on the list, and at the same time, faculty members were also asked to provide any information on the career outcomes of these individuals as well. This effort took place during the first 2 weeks of December 2015. The final step in the process involved entering the continuing education program enrollment information of those individuals who were removed prior to step one into the data-collection system.

As mentioned in Figure 2.1, each of the data sources provides different amounts of career outcomes data with the steps near the beginning of the process providing the most data as compared to the steps toward the end of the collection period. Figure 2.2 summarizes the data-collection steps as a flow chart and indicates the number of respondents collected from each effort.

Resources/Tools.   The collection of career outcomes data is a resource-intensive process involving personnel, money, time, and tools. As previously mentioned, a number of offices collaborate in this effort, but institutional research's primarily responsibility is data entry, tracking, and organization. A full-time institutional research data analyst coordinates a bulk of the data collection. Additionally, a graduate student manages the telephone-calling effort by hiring and training undergraduate student callers, coordinating the use of space in the career center, and supervising the evening calling sessions. There are monetary costs to the data collection, mainly in the form of incentives to complete the Web survey (e.g.,

Figure 2.2. Flowchart of Data-Collection Steps and Number of Responses

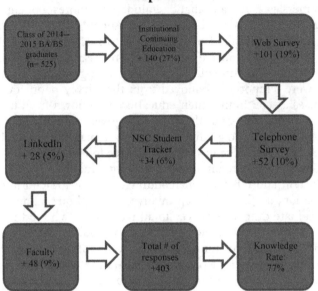

gift cards worth about $200), work-study funds to pay the undergraduate students, and costs associated with providing food to the student callers. The Qualtrics survey form was also used as the centralized data-entry tool to keep track of the multiple sources of data that were also collected at different time points. Two validation fields, consisting of student ID number and last name, were required to access the survey in order to prevent against duplicate entries. For the Web survey, recent graduates supplied this information at the beginning of the survey, and for the calling effort, undergraduate callers inputted this information as they administered the survey via telephone. For the information received from institutional records, NSC StudentTracker, LinkedIn, and faculty, the institutional research office entered these data into the Qualtrics survey form. As previously mentioned, data from these latter sources, at the bare minimum, contained the current career status of the graduates (i.e., employed, enrolled in continuing education, etc.) but additional information, such as salary, was not available.

Analysis and Reporting.   Descriptive analysis was used to summarize the knowledge rates and career outcomes rates for the Class of 2014–2015 based on the current status of individuals. For undergraduate degree recipients, the knowledge rate was 77%, and for graduate degree recipients, it was 71% (Table 2.1). Both of these figures meet the 65% threshold as recommended by NACE. The career outcomes rate, which includes the proportion of graduates employed, enrolled in graduate/professional school, military service, or in volunteer service, was 96% for undergraduate degree

Table 2.1. Knowledge and Career Outcomes Rates

Status	BA/BS degree recipients		Masters/Doctoral recipients		Total	
	n	%	n	%	n	%
Employed Full-Time	155	38%	258	85%	413	58%
Employed Part-Time	23	6%	16	5%	39	6%
Enrolled in graduate/ professional school	203	50%	20	7%	223	32%
Military Service	1	0%	1	0%	2	0%
Seeking Employment	9	2%	7	2%	16	2%
Seeking Continuing Education	7	2%	1	0%	8	1%
Volunteer Service	4	1%	0	0%	4	1%
Not Seeking Employment	1	0%	1	0%	2	0%
Total	403	100%	304	100%	707	100%
Total # of Graduates	525		430		955	
Knowledge Rate	**77%**		**71%**		**74%**	
Career Outcomes Rate*	**96%**		**97%**		**96%**	

*Excludes "seeking employment," "seeking continuing education," and "not seeking employment."

recipients and 97% for graduate degree recipients (Table 2.1). Additional analysis included summarizing the data for items pertaining to employer name, job title, graduate school name, graduate program, employment sector, and salary.

An official college publication was also created in conjunction with the offices of enrollment management, marketing and communications, and academic deans. In this report, the institutional-level data were presented at the school and program levels. Table 2.2 shows an example of how these

Table 2.2. Example of Career Outcomes Data for the School of Health, Physical Education, & Recreation

Bachelor's Career Outcomes—School Level	
Employed	67%
Enrolled in Graduate School	27%
Total Career Outcomes	94%
Knowledge Rate (based on 108 responses)	64%
Bachelor's Career Outcomes—Sport Management Major	
Employed	85%
Enrolled Graduate School	5%
Total Career Outcomes	90%
Knowledge Rate	69%

data were broken out at these additional levels of analysis for the School of Health, Physical Education, and Recreation. Undergraduate degree recipients in the graduating class for this school had a knowledge rate of 64% and a career outcomes rate of 94%. Examination of the results for one of the academic majors in this school, reveals the knowledge rate of sport management majors was 69% with a career outcomes rate of 90% (Table 2.2). In addition, the publication was designed for an external audience and included a list of sample employers, employment titles, and graduate school names and programs also broken out at the academic major level.

Interpreting and Using Results.   The institutional-level results pertaining to the overall knowledge and career outcomes rates are used as institutional effectiveness measures. For example, the undergraduate career outcomes rate was reported in regional accreditation reports. As indicated in Table 2.1, the institutional-level results indicate that out of the 403 individuals with known statuses, 203 or 50% of the BA/BS recipients are enrolled in a graduate or professional school. This large proportion of students continuing their education is mostly explained by three dual-degree professional programs (i.e., occupation therapy, physician assistant, and physical therapy) offered at this institution in which students receive a bachelor's degree in 4 years on their way to completing their master's or doctoral degree requirements. Approximately 140 of those 203 undergraduates at Springfield College continue their education in one of these dual-degree programs. Although this outcome is institution-specific, it speaks to the importance of interpreting postgraduate outcomes data within the context on institutional mission and type. As mentioned in Chapter 1, the College Scorecard, which was released by the U.S. Department of Education in September 2015, made waves by linking individual Internal Revenue System (IRS) information with federal aid data to report median salary information of an institution's graduates. Yet, this earnings information is but one slice of a school's postgraduate outcome pie. For this institution, the other big slice is the number of undergraduates continuing their education in graduate or professional school. The high percentage of continuing education students is also evident when compared to the inaugural national data report compiled by NACE of those institutions who shared their data in 2014. In this report, 190 schools shared data of approximately 266,000 bachelor's degree recipients, and approximately 16% of these graduates continued their education (NACE, 2015). Among private-not-for-profit institutions, the national figure is 18%; thus, this institution's continuing education figure of 50% is much higher than its national peers.

The school- and program-level results are used and shared in a number of different settings. First, school deans and department chairs used the detailed career outcomes rates by academic major level for program accreditation report and academic program review. The official publication is also shared with prospective students and their families at open houses and recruiting fairs by the office of enrollment management. Along these lines, the official report is useful for answering inquiries about the job prospects for students who major in a specific major. Finally, the career center also uses the report to assist in the advising and counseling of current students about potential postgraduate career outcomes.

Challenges

Despite the improved data collection of postgraduate outcomes, several challenges still remain. Although the use of multiple data sources has increased the knowledge rate of recent graduates, salary information is still lacking. Unlike the College Scorecard, this effort relies on the self-reporting of one's yearly earnings, and this institution has struggled to capture a reasonable number of data points. Part of the reason stems from the fact that, as previously noted, half of the respondents are continuing their education, which is an important outcome by itself given the strong professional programs offered by the institution. Another challenge is that despite having a knowledge rate of over 75%, it may not be useful or appropriate to break out career statuses for those academic majors with a small number of undergraduate degree recipients. A final challenge to this process is the amount of time it takes to coordinate the collaborating offices, personnel, data sources, and analysis. It is roughly a 6-month process starting with creating the survey form and defining the population in September to the publication of the results in March.

Lessons Learned

From a practical perspective, there are important takeaways for an institutional research office embarking on this data collection. The most important piece is to collaborate with offices and departments that also have an interest in using this information. This is the best way to reach the minimum 65% knowledge rate NACE recommends. In particular, working with faculty has been instrumental, as some students prefer to maintain their connection to their academic advisors and professors after graduation rather than the institution as a whole. This makes faculty members a useful resource in learning about the current status of some recent graduates. Furthermore, academic deans can encourage faculty to assist in the data collection and emphasize that more career outcomes data means a more complete picture of their graduates when broken out at the major level. An equally important aspect of collecting postgraduate outcomes information is for institutional research to be the central repository of all the data. Although this can be burdensome, institutional researchers are in the best position to track and analyze these data systematically. Given the lengthy timeline of this process, planning ahead is also crucial, especially in terms of scheduling the different data-collection steps. At Springfield College, the goal is to have all the data entered into Qualtrics by December 31. Working backward from this date, the data-collection steps are then scheduled accordingly. Finally, though the process is lengthy and weighted heavily on the data collection, the final results and reporting should not be an afterthought. Questions such as how the data will be presented, who is the audience, and how information will be used, especially in conjunction with other institutional outcomes data, should be discussed early in the process.

References

National Association of Colleges and Employers. (2014). *Standards and protocols for the collection and dissemination of graduating student initial career outcomes information for undergraduates* [PDF File]. Retrieved from http://www.naceweb.org/uploadedFiles/Pages/advocacy/first-destination-survey-standards-and-protocols.pdf

National Association of Colleges and Employers. (2015). *First destinations for the college class of 2015* [PDF File]. Retrieved from http://www.naceweb.org/uploadedFiles/Pages/surveys/first-destination/nace-first-destination-survey-final-report-05-2015.pdf

Rogers, M. (2013, December 17). Job placement confusion. *Inside Higher Ed.* Retrieved from https://www.insidehighered.com/news/2013/12/17/colleges-report-job-outcomes-results-are-limited-value

The Carnegie Classification of Institutions of Higher Education. (n.d.). *About Carnegie Classification.* Retrieved from http://carnegieclassifications.iu.edu/

The Institute for College Access and Success. (2014). *Student debt and the class of 2014.* Retrieved from http://ticas.org/sites/default/files/pub_files/classof2014.pdf

JEROLD S. LAGUILLES *is the director of institutional research at Springfield College.*

3

Comprehensive data are essential to answer questions from prospective students, parents, and private and public entities about the cost of college and students' return on investment, as well as to demonstrate how colleges and universities are helping to prepare the future workforce. An evolutionary data-collection process, efforts to improve the distribution of results, and implications will be discussed to inform public research universities hoping to begin or refine a first-destination survey.

First-Destination Outcomes at a Public Research University: Aligning Our Survey With a Set of Standards

Heather A. Kelly, Allison M. Walters

It is imperative to provide more complete data to answer questions from prospective students, parents, and private and public entities about the cost of college and students' return on investment, as well as demonstrating how colleges and universities are helping to prepare the future workforce. The University of California at Los Angeles (UCLA) Higher Education Research Institute (HERI) Cooperative Institutional Research Program (CIRP) has been collecting the expectations of entering first-year students for 50 years. The *Chronicle of Higher Education* published an interactive tool to explore the CIRP data at http://chronicle.com/interactives/freshmen-survey. Now more than ever, college students indicate that being able to get a better job is very important in deciding to go to college (70.0% in 1971 compared to 85.2% in 2015 with a high of 87.9% in 2012) (Kueppers, 2016). In addition, more than half of the college student respondents indicate that preparing for graduate or professional school is a very important reason in deciding to go to college (58.8% in 2015 compared to 34.8% in 1971 with a high of 61.9% in 2012) (Kueppers, 2016).

A metric that can address all of the above concerns is the first destination of our college graduates. However, the only way this metric can be communicated accurately and effectively to prospective students, parents, and other stakeholders to help demonstrate the value of a college education is by increasing the volume and reliability of the information being gathered.

NEW DIRECTIONS FOR INSTITUTIONAL RESEARCH, no. 169 © 2016 Wiley Periodicals, Inc.
Published online in Wiley Online Library (wileyonlinelibrary.com) • DOI: 10.1002/ir.20168

This chapter will present strategies employed by a public research university to adopt the National Association of Colleges and Employers (NACE) standards, survey data elements, and administrative timeline to collect first-destination outcomes of graduating students and attain the recommended 65% knowledge rate for bachelor's degree recipients. The evolutionary data-collection process and efforts to improve the distribution of results will be discussed, as well as implications for other public research universities hoping to begin or refine a first-destination survey. Although institutional research (IR) collects outcomes data for all of our graduates, this chapter will focus on the outcomes of our bachelor's degree graduates.

The Career Plans Survey Early Years

IR has been charged by Career Services to collect and analyze postgraduation activities for its graduates for over 40 years. Employment data for graduates can be found in our University Archives dating back to 1974. The University yielded a survey response rate of 23% in 1985 and the highest response rate of 47% in 2002. The data-collection process was straightforward. Before the emergence of Web surveys, graduates were mailed a paper survey to complete. More recently, the data-collection process had two steps: (a) a survey card was distributed at six of the seven college convocations in May and (b) a Qualtrics Web survey was administered in November and the following May. The goal was to understand what our college graduates were doing a full year after graduation. The Class of 2013 Career Plans Survey response rate was 34%. IR and Career Services have always been cognizant of our response rates and now our senior administration is paying very close attention.

Overview of NACE First-Destination Survey Initiative

The Provost's Executive Council is very much aware of the shifting expectations of stakeholders, increasing costs of higher education, return on investment concerns among students and families, the need to demonstrate higher education's ability to prepare a future workforce, and the U.S. Department of Education College Scorecard. In March 2014, the Council charged that an annual Career Outcomes Survey will incorporate NACE standards and protocols in collecting first-destination outcomes of graduating students and attain the recommended 65% knowledge rate for bachelor's degree recipients in the class of 2015. NACE (2014) defines knowledge rate as the percent of graduates for which the institution has reasonable and verifiable information concerning the graduates' postgraduation career activities. This information may come directly from the graduate or obtained via other sources, such as online profiles, employers, or parents.

NEW DIRECTIONS FOR INSTITUTIONAL RESEARCH • DOI: 10.1002/ir

The Council acknowledged NACE's national role in benchmarking these data and its advocacy role in key legislative issues such as the U.S. Department of Education's College Affordability and Transparency Center College Scorecard employment metric. Benefits of incorporating the NACE standards into our data-collection efforts include defining the graduating class, targeted knowledge rates, career outcomes reporting categories, a career outcomes rate, a timeline for summary data collection and reporting, and ability to pursue further assessments (NACE, 2014). This allows us to improve data-collection efforts and be more accountable and transparent. In addition, it provides the ability to benchmark career outcomes with other higher education institutions, which will be of particular interest to our many stakeholders. In the spring 2014, IR launched a pilot test and adopted NACE's standards, survey data elements, and the administration timeline. NACE's knowledge-rate recommendations were also incorporated.

Revising the Class of 2014 Career Plans Survey

Institutional Research and Career Services set out to develop a plan to achieve a 50% knowledge rate for the bachelor's class of 2014 Career Plans Survey with an eye on achieving a 65% knowledge rate for the class of 2015. The goal was to align our survey and time frame with NACE's standards (NACE, 2014). IR would enhance efforts to improve the 35% response rate from previous years to a 50% knowledge rate in 2014. IR decided to embrace 2014 as a pilot year, and use it as a learning experience to build campus-wide support and utilize NACE's recommended knowledge-rate data sources of the National Student Clearinghouse (NSC) and LinkedIn in addition to our standard survey efforts. IR would not submit data to the 2014 NACE First-Destination Survey but planned to build upon our successes in the pilot year and improve efforts where necessary in 2015 to achieve the recommended 65% knowledge rate and participate in the 2015 NACE First-Destination Survey.

IR and the Director of Career Services began planning for the Class of 2014 Career Plans Survey in early spring 2014 by updating convocation survey card and Qualtrics survey to reflect the NACE survey standards. Figure 3.1 shows the front and back of the Class of 2014 Career Plans Survey card, which was distributed to graduates attending the College of Engineering's May 2014 convocation. The Qualtrics survey included all of the same questions on this survey card and would be distributed to all graduates in fall 2014. There were fewer questions presented to the respondents of the Qualtrics survey because the Qualtrics survey incorporated display logic to show only relevant follow-up questions based on how a respondent answered Question A "Which of the following BEST describes your PRIMARY status after graduation?"

Figure 3.1. Class of 2014 Career Plans Survey Card Revised with NACE Standard Questions (Front and Back)

UNIVERSITY OF DELAWARE
COLLEGE OF ENGINEERING
2014 Post-Graduation Activities Survey

The University is seeking information about your post-graduation plans. This information assists several offices in planning programs and services. All responses are confidential. Please complete the survey and return it with your name card or leave it on your seat.

Name: _____

UD ID: _____

Post-Graduation email address: _____

Gender: 1. Male 2. Female

Residence status while at UD: 1. Resident 2. Non Resident

Student status: 1. Undergraduate 2. Graduate

Degree date: 1. Fall 2. Winter 3. Spring 4. Summer

Degree(s) received: _____

Major: _____

A. Which of the following BEST describes your PRIMARY status after graduation? Please select only ONE of the following categories:
   1. **Employed full-time** (on average 30 hours or more per week)
   2. **Employed part-time** (on average less than 30 hours per week)
   3. Participating in a **volunteer or service program** (e.g., Peace Corps). Please provide details below:
   Organization _____
   Assignment location-city, state, and country _____

   Role or title _____
   4. Serving in the **U.S. Military**. Please provide details below:
   Service Branch _____
   Rank _____
   5. Enrolled in a program of continuing education
   6. Seeking employment
   7. Planning to continue education but not yet enrolled
   8. Not seeking employment or continuing education at this time

UNIVERSITYof DELAWARE.

Please turn over for additional questions

Class of 2014 Survey Efforts

Once IR updated the survey instrument to comply with NACE standards, IR worked with the Director of Career Services to revise the survey administration timeline. In past years, IR collaborated with contacts in six of the seven colleges. These six colleges (all but Arts & Sciences, because of its large size) hold college convocation ceremonies during commencement weekend each May. College contacts distribute survey cards and pencils to graduates in the staging area prior to the opening procession, encourage graduates to complete the survey, and collect the cards to forward to IR for data entry and analysis. IR knew from experience that these surveys administered at the convocations achieve the highest response rate due to the

NEW DIRECTIONS FOR INSTITUTIONAL RESEARCH • DOI: 10.1002/ir

Figure 3.1. *Continued.*

"captive audience" environment. Follow-up surveys 3, 6, 9, and 12 months postconvocation receive lower response rates; however, they do offer increased potential for a graduate to have secured postgraduate employment or educational plans, which many graduates do not yet have in May at convocation. Given the high response rates typical at convocation and knowing that survey follow-up efforts would be enhanced in 2014, IR decided to continue the college convocation survey administration as the first data-collection effort for the class of 2014. IR also worked with the Honors Program to administer the survey cards during their Honors Program graduation event, and one department in the College of Health Sciences that decided to send their graduates a Qualtrics survey invitation in early May instead of administering cards at their convocation. Career

NEW DIRECTIONS FOR INSTITUTIONAL RESEARCH • DOI: 10.1002/ir

Services also placed a link to the Qualtrics survey on their alumni services page.

IR and Career Services created a timeline for the follow-up survey administration reflective of NACE's timeline, with the goal to complete survey data collection and all knowledge rate efforts by December 31, 2014. IR would administer three follow-up surveys, one at the beginning of each month of September, October, and November 2014. A high-profile administrator at the University addressed each of the surveys: the September follow-up came from the President, October's from graduates' respective Deans, and November's from both the Director of Career Services and the Vice President of Development and Alumni Relations. Career Services purchased an iPad Mini as an incentive for the September follow-up survey. IR highlighted this new incentive and posted an announcement with the survey link to the campus news service, which reaches alumni in a daily digest. The announcement and the President's invite e-mail explained that those who completed the survey in September were eligible for a drawing for an iPad Mini. IR sent the September survey to all class of 2014 bachelor's degree recipients ($n = 3,747$).

To prepare for the October follow-up survey from the Deans, IR merged the Qualtrics survey data from September into the master file containing the convocation results. Because IR staff spent the summer months validating and entering the convocation card data, they could then look for duplicate respondent records and keep the graduates' more recent response. In many cases, this means that a respondent completing a convocation survey card in May indicated that they were "seeking employment" but their September response indicates that they are now "employed full-time." After removing the previous response, IR then prepared the October survey population file. This file did not contain those that were "employed full-time" or "enrolled in a program of continuing education." IR sent the October follow-up survey to the remaining respondents plus all other nonrespondents from the original class of 2014 population file. IR utilized this same process for administering the final follow-up survey in November, which came from both the Director of Career Services and the Vice President of Development and Alumni Relations. This particular follow-up survey invitation emphasized that this was the last time graduates could provide data and indicated the survey would close in 2 weeks. Table 3.1 shows the response rates achieved

Table 3.1. Response Rates for 2014 Career Plans Survey—Convocation Through November Follow-Up Survey

	May Convocation Cards/Qualtrics	September Qualtrics	October Qualtrics	November Qualtrics
N	883	538	132	87
Individual response rate	23.6%	14.4%	3.5%	2.3%
Cumulative response rate	23.6%	38.0%	41.5%	43.8%

NEW DIRECTIONS FOR INSTITUTIONAL RESEARCH • DOI: 10.1002/ir

from the survey efforts from convocation through the November follow-up survey. Note that these are final survey counts and response rates after removing all duplicate respondents. Actual yields for each survey were larger because they contained duplicate responses that were later removed.

Class of 2014 Knowledge Rate Efforts

In past years, the Career Plans Survey efforts only utilized surveys to collect data on our graduates. Response rates in the 30–35% range were attained even with the convocation cards surveying six of seven colleges and Qualtrics follow-up surveys 3, 6, 9, and even 12 months postgraduation. In 2014, however, IR aimed to follow the NACE standards as a pilot effort to raise the response/knowledge rate and to create comparable results to the NACE benchmarks they planned to publish in June 2015. One area that was new for us was the effort to gather data from NACE-approved knowledge-rate data sources: the NSC and LinkedIn. IR and Career Services agreed that IR would obtain subsequent enrollment data from the NSC for any of our graduate nonrespondents to know where they may be enrolled in a program of continuing education. Career Services agreed to complete the LinkedIn searches in December on the remaining nonrespondents or those who indicated they were "seeking employment" on the survey.

After the November follow-up survey had been live for 2 weeks, IR closed the survey and merged the November follow-up survey results into the master file. IR then submitted a subsequent enrollment request to the NSC containing all those graduates from the class of 2014 who did not respond to the survey. After reviewing the NSC results, 300 new records were added. IR added these new records to the survey data, which brought the total knowledge rate to 52%.

In late November 2014, IR provided Career Services with two files for their LinkedIn searches. One file contained all survey nonrespondents and one file contained those respondents who last indicated that they were seeking employment. Career Services had intended to assign the LinkedIn search project to several staff members and student employees; however, because of a number of circumstances including the departure of the Director of Career Services, they were unable to complete this project. IR was pleased that the 52% knowledge rate exceeded our goal of a 50% knowledge rate for the 2014 pilot year. IR was curious, however, about the effect of any LinkedIn results. For a few weeks in spring 2015, an IR graduate student employee completed LinkedIn searches and added 325 new records, bringing the knowledge rate to 61%. Finally—and although not aligned with the NACE standards and timeline for the class of 2014 survey—IR sent one last survey follow-up in June 2015 requesting updates to graduates' postgraduation status, and yielded 47 more records, bringing the knowledge rate to 61.7%. Table 3.2 shows the additional records and knowledge rates added from the knowledge-rate efforts and final survey effort for the class of 2014.

**Table 3.2. Knowledge Rates for 2014 Career Plans
Survey—Knowledge Rate Efforts**

	Through November Qualtrics	National Student Clearinghouse	LinkedIn Searches	June Qualtrics
N	1,640	300	325	47
Individual knowledge rate	43.8%	8.0%	8.7%	1.2%
Cumulative knowledge rate	43.8%	51.8%	60.5%	61.7%

Class of 2014 Results

Overall, the Class of 2014 Career Plans Survey results were very positive. Table 3.3 shows a comparison of results from 2010 through 2014. Unlike the previous methodology, IR followed NACE standards and included all "seeking employment" results gathered at convocation, unless they were updated by a later survey response. Because of this, the 2014 rate of "seeking employment" responses increased by approximately nine percentage points from 2013, and the "full-time employment" responses fell by the same nine points. When examining our results and the overall 2014 NACE First-Destination Survey benchmarks, our results are comparable and only slightly lower than NACE's on "full-time employment" (53.1% vs. 55.4%) and "part-time employment" (5.4% vs. 6.6%), whereas they are lower for "seeking employment" (10.2% vs. 13.9%) (NACE, 2015). The results are most favorable when comparing our Career Outcomes Rate of 87.2% versus the NACE average of 80.3%. NACE (2015) defines Career Outcomes Rate as "the number of graduates who have landed in either any of the employment categories plus service and military plus continuing education divided by the number of students for whom an outcome is known" (p. 6). Overall, our pilot year results were very promising and showed that the University compared quite favorably with NACE benchmarks. IR was pleased to reach a 62% knowledge rate, but given the difficulty adhering to the NACE timeline of data collection and knowledge rate efforts, IR began earnestly planning for the Class of 2015 Career Plans Survey with the intention of improving our survey methodology and streamlining our knowledge-rate efforts.

Class of 2015 Career Plans Survey

In preparation for the Class of 2015 convocation in May 2015, IR reached out to college and Honors Program contacts and all of them again agreed to participate in administering the convocation survey card to their graduates. In addition to arranging for the six colleges and the Honors Program to administer survey cards at their convocation events, IR also provided the Qualtrics survey link and requested they send it out to their graduates in any e-mail communication concerning graduation. This resulted in some

Table 3.3. Career Plans Survey Results 2010–2014

Year	Number in Class	Response/ Knowledge Rate	Full-Time Employment	Part-Time Employment	Further Education	Military	Seeking Employment
2014	3,747	61.7%	53.1%	5.4%	27.5%	0.4%	10.2%
2013	3,741	33.7%	61.6%	7.6%	25.0%	0.7%	1.4%
2012	3,535	35.8%	62.9%	7.3%	24.4%	0.9%	2.7%
2011	3,621	33.3%	62.9%	8.5%	24.0%	0.7%	2.2%
2010	3,361	27.3%	59.0%	8.9%	26.0%	0.9%	2.2%

colleges publicizing the Qualtrics survey in addition to administering the convocation survey cards and one unit within the College of Health Sciences using only the survey link for their data collection. For the first time, IR reached out to the College of Arts and Sciences, which is the largest college with numerous departmental convocation ceremonies. The College provided their graduation list for IR to send the Qualtrics survey to their students. These efforts resulted in a great response, and once the September follow-up survey was complete (again with an invitation from the President and with an iPad Mini incentive) and the October follow-up survey from the Deans was accomplished, a 52.3% response rate was attained, more than a 10 percentage point increase compared to the same phase of the 2014 survey. Given the low response to the 2014 November follow-up from the Career Services Director and the Vice President of Development and Alumni Relations, the Interim Director of Career Services requested IR send the November follow-up from each graduate's Career Services liaison. This liaison specializes in certain majors and requested that graduates complete the survey while also making themselves available for any resume review or counseling services needed during graduates' job search. The November follow-up survey brought the response rate up to 55.3%, nearly 12 percentage points higher than after the November follow-up in 2014.

As IR began to plan for the knowledge-rate efforts, the new Director of Career Services arrived and was eager to add value to our efforts. When reviewing the 2014 pilot year results, he saw the opportunity to invest more time in the LinkedIn searches, as well as reach out to campus units to solicit data from faculty and departmental service staff. As IR completed the subsequent enrollment request to the NSC, the new Director began meeting with college and Honors Program staff, department chairs, and athletics staff to build new relationships and assistance in gathering available data for a more complete picture of the class of 2015. The NSC request yielded 255 new records and brought the knowledge rate to 61.8%.

The new Director spent the month of December completing LinkedIn searches on nonrespondents and those respondents who last indicated they were seeking employment. His efforts had a great impact on our results: when adding in new records and updates to previous responses from LinkedIn, along with internal data from the Honors Program, the College of Business and Economics, and the School of Education reached a knowledge rate of 70.1%. This total includes some LinkedIn searches conducted by IR student employees and also a final survey sent to the College of Arts & Sciences graduates in December.

The results of the 2015 Career Plans Survey are extremely positive. IR learned from our experiences in 2014 and created a collaborative plan with the new Director of Career Services. His engagement and contribution to the knowledge rate efforts and data verification process not only increased the knowledge rate more than eight percentage points from 61.7% to 70.1% within the NACE standard timeline, but led to more complete data for each record and resulted in more records being turned over from "still seeking" or "employed part-time" to "employed full-time." He used much of his time in January 2016 to verify the records with the use of LinkedIn and employer Web sites. NACE's results of the 2015 First-Destination Survey will not be published until June 2016; however, Table 3.4 shows how our 2015 results have improved when compared with our 2014 results and the 2014 NACE results. Our "full-time employment" rate increased approximately 10 percentage points from 2014, while the "part-time employment" and "seeking employment" rates decreased by nearly three and four percentage points, respectively. The Career Outcomes Rate—the summary statistic describing the overall percentage of those with a positive career outcome— reflects the overall improvement in our results from 2014 to 2015 with an increase of more than four percentage points to 91.5%.

Challenges and Considerations

Although our efforts in 2014 and 2015 have led to improved knowledge rates and more accurate and complete data on our graduates, it is worth noting the many challenges involved in our efforts to achieve these results. First and foremost, these improved data-collection efforts result in a heavier workload that involves many individuals across campus. The key challenge is the amount and time and attention involved to complete this survey within the NACE timeline. IR is pleased to have the "captive audience" at convocation, but the hard-copy cards require several months to code, verify, and enter data from the approximately 1,700 cards returned to us. In the future, IR may consider asking graduates to complete the survey on their mobile device instead of the cards to save time on coding and data entry.

It's also important to plan for the turnaround time to download, clean, and merge the follow-up survey data sets into the master file. IR performs this before each follow-up survey, removes duplicate records, and creates the follow-up survey population file with nonrespondents and those graduates "seeking employment." Given the complexity involved in handling these data, IR prefers to manage these survey data and follow-up administrations itself.

Career Services took the lead on the LinkedIn searches, and noted the significant time investment to perform hundreds of individual searches. Career Services also noted that LinkedIn profiles should be read with a careful eye to be certain that the profile actually belongs to the graduate in question. Career Services spent time considering whether the employment information was indeed postgraduate employment. They also found it was sometimes necessary to search for additional employer details, like city or state, where these were not provided in the profile. IR is grateful for Career Services' willingness to collaborate and their contributions as IR time and resources could not accommodate these additional efforts.

NEW DIRECTIONS FOR INSTITUTIONAL RESEARCH • DOI: 10.1002/ir

Table 3.4. 2015 Career Plans Survey Results Compared to 2014 Results and 2014 NACE Overall Benchmark

Year	Number in Class	Response/ Knowledge Rate	Full-Time Employment	Part-Time Employment	Further Education	Military	Seeking Employment
2015	3,956	70.1%	62.7%	2.6%	24.8%	0.4%	6.4%
2014	3,747	61.7%	53.1%	5.4%	27.5%	0.4%	10.2%
NACE 2014	266,119	65.7%	55.4%	6.6%	16.4%	0.8%	13.9%

Relationship building among the various colleges, departments, and units around campus also requires significant investment. Our new Director of Career Services has taken a proactive role in this area and continues to collaborate with these individuals to help them see the benefit of having robust outcomes data and therefore encourage their graduates' participation. This again poses a challenge for IR to provide clean data quickly after the data-collection process closes. Increasingly, campus colleagues desire real-time results during the process, creating an even larger burden on IR to not only manage but continually communicate results during the data-collection process. Career Services may consider a tool like 12Twenty (www.12twenty.com), which offers an online suite to meet these needs while also offering analytics and reporting capabilities. Presently, Career Services is considering best practices for data reporting and dissemination. One example is developing infographics to summarize overall postgraduate outcomes, as well as by college as seen in Figure 3.2. In addition, they are collaborating with senior administration, admissions, and IR to

Figure 3.2. Postgraduation Outcomes Infographic for the College of Business and Economics

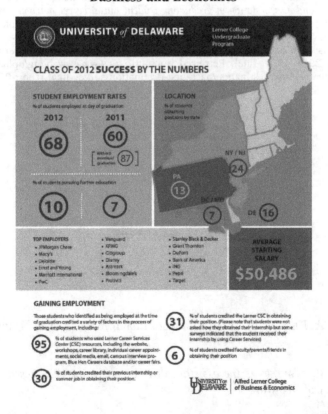

determine how to create a dynamic Web portal for users to drill down to postgraduation outcomes by college, department, and major.

Department leaders, senior administrators, state officials, and the public see the value in accessing detailed employment and graduate school outcomes data for our graduates. These data provide a means to be accountable and transparent to a variety of external stakeholders, in addition to supporting internal stakeholders' student advising, program recruitment and reporting efforts. The key to success is broader involvement beyond institutional research and career services while maintaining a centralized data-collection hub. Although collecting first-destination career outcomes data is a complex and labor-intensive venture, the ability to demonstrate the value of a college education is well worth the effort!

References

Kueppers, C. (2016, February 11). Today's freshman class is the most likely to protest in half a century. *The Chronicle of Higher Education*. Retrieved February 29, 2016, from http://chronicle.com/article/Today-s-Freshman-Class-Is/235273?cid=at&utm_source=at&utm_medium=en&elq=fcf08a84c37844abaf4730f6e29c5384&elqCampaignId=2420&elqaid=7858&elqat=1&elqTrackId=ea9326aab1a3499aa5bf0efe9fd69180

National Association of Colleges and Employers. (2014). *Standards and protocols for the collection and dissemination of graduating student initial career outcomes information for undergraduates*. [PDF File]. Retrieved from http://www.naceweb.org/uploadedFiles/Pages/advocacy/first-destination-survey-standards-and-protocols.pdf

National Association of Colleges and Employers. (2015). *First destinations for the college class of 2015*. [PDF File]. Retrieved from http://www.naceweb.org/uploadedFiles/Pages/surveys/first-destination/nace-first-destination-survey-final-report-05-2015.pdf

HEATHER A. KELLY *is the director of institutional research at the University of Delaware.*

ALLISON M. WALTERS *is the assistant director of institutional research at the University of Delaware.*

NEW DIRECTIONS FOR INSTITUTIONAL RESEARCH • DOI: 10.1002/ir

4

This chapter explores case studies from four private liberal arts colleges with different approaches to expanding the college "value proposition" to include the values of a liberal education.

So Much More than Salary: Outcomes Research in the Liberal Arts

Cate Rowen

The national conversation about higher education outcomes has focused heavily on the economic results of degrees for individuals. Although alumni careers and financial independence are obviously of critical importance for our institutions, private liberal arts colleges share the aspiration to prepare students for broader postgraduate outcomes.

With the release of the College Scorecard in 2015, the federal government has firmly staked out the importance of postgraduate earnings as a key measure of college success by just three metrics: cost of attendance, graduation rate, and postgraduate salary. College Scorecard validates the "return on investment" rhetoric put forward by the website PayScale.com, which ranks colleges and universities based on their cost of attendance in relation to the self-reported postgraduate earnings they collect from their own website users (PayScale, 2016). Also in 2015, presidential candidate Marco Rubio claimed that welders made more money than philosophers. This claim was widely debunked (Kessler, 2015), but the statement encourages the myth that investing in liberal arts education is a luxury reserved for those who do not need to make a living. Representatives of the liberal arts sector have had mixed success in countering this narrative. The American Association of Colleges and Universities (AAC&U) has done significant work in this area through its Liberal Education and America's Promise (LEAP) initiative, identifying essential learning outcomes for college students and connecting these to employment as well as citizenship and life satisfaction (Finley, 2012). Yet, the narrative continues in politics and in the press that philosophy and English majors will have their futures limited to careers making coffee and living in their parents' basements (Goudreau, 2012).

Given this environment, it is difficult for institutional leaders to reframe the conversation in a way that is consistent with the goals of the

New Directions for Institutional Research, no. 169 © 2016 Wiley Periodicals, Inc.
Published online in Wiley Online Library (wileyonlinelibrary.com) • DOI: 10.1002/ir.20169

liberal arts. If we push back too hard on the employment and earnings discussion, we risk taking an elitist and impractical position that may be abrasive to the parents paying tuition bills. Yet if we allow the conversation about higher education to be focused on earnings, we lose the opportunity to promote the benefits of a liberal arts education that define our institutional missions and our educational values. It is difficult, however, to reframe a discussion based on such concrete concepts as dollars and cents into one that treads into such ethereal territory as lifelong learning, intercultural capacity, and citizenship.

Defining the Ineffable

Institutional researchers have an opportunity to help frame the national conversation about educational value by contextualizing institutional earnings outcome data from sources like College Scorecard and PayScale with data about the broader aims of the liberal arts. Through collaboration with faculty leaders, data stewards, and IR colleagues, we can help to frame research that can provide our institutions with evidence-based rebuttals to public narratives that reduce higher education to exclusively monetary terms. Supplementing research that tracks the concrete employment outcomes of our students, we can expand our inquiry to explore the ways in which a liberal arts education supported the broader promise of a liberal arts education.

One of the most challenging components of any assessment effort is bringing stakeholders to consensus about desired outcomes. This is never truer than when one is faced with doing it at the scale of the entire liberal arts education. Institutional researchers have a variety of tools at their disposal to glean outcomes concepts. Strategic plans, self-studies, learning outcomes, and promotional material all include aspirational statements about what we believe represents a liberal arts education. Some liberal arts institutions have clearly identified their visions of the postgraduate outcomes of the liberal arts, and have embedded them in mission statements or general education outcomes. Yet in many cases, the future-oriented outcomes of the liberal arts may be deeply held without being concretely articulated.

In cases where liberal arts outcomes have not been identified, AAC&U's LEAP Initiative's essential learning outcomes provide a national consensus framework to start a campus-based discussion or even to guide initial research that can be used to spark subsequent conversation. The LEAP initiative frames specific educational outcomes that support college graduates who "need higher levels of learning and knowledge as well as strong intellectual and practical skills to navigate this more demanding environment successfully and responsibly" (AAC&U, 2014).

NEW DIRECTIONS FOR INSTITUTIONAL RESEARCH • DOI: 10.1002/ir

Examples of Assessment Beyond Salary

It is clear that there is no simple set of metrics that describe the deeper aspirations of the liberal arts. This gives institutional researchers a unique opportunity to explore ways to collect information from our graduates that expands the dialogue about what success looks like for graduates of liberal arts colleges. The following sections profile four very different approaches to researching liberal arts outcomes. The aims of the projects vary, ranging from exploratory qualitative research based in appreciative inquiry at Hampshire College to a large institutional initiative integrating disparate data sources into an analytic data warehouse at Carleton. Given that no consensus approach yet exists, these case studies are offered not as fixed solutions, but instead are meant to provide inspiration and ideas to institutional research (IR) practitioners who will continue the process of measuring the impact of liberal arts in the world.

Cohort Surveys at Smith College

Smith is the nation's largest liberal arts women's college with about 2,500 undergraduate students. A highly selective institution and one of the former seven sisters, it is known for its commitment to access, with more than one-fifth of its students receiving Pell grants, and more than half receiving institutional aid. Smith students pursue majors in more than 50 areas of study through 44 departments and interdisciplinary programs, as well as courses through four other institutions in its Five College Consortium (Smith College, 2016).

Smith's outcomes research initiative represents a broad institutional effort to be more systematic and timely in collecting information from alumni. Like others, facing new demands from accreditation and even more pressing expectations from funding sources for detailed, accurate data about student outcomes, we identified a need to coordinate our data-collection efforts to capture information about student outcomes broadly, including employment, postbaccalaureate education, and assessment of preparation in core liberal arts capacities, among other things.

In 2009, we brought together separate initiatives from Institutional Research and Career Development to conduct annual alumnae surveys at fixed points postgraduation. In the past, IR and Career Development had queried alumnae at different times with different objectives. Although there was some collaboration before 2009, coordinating efforts provided an opportunity to make the most of every alumnae survey opportunity. Perhaps more importantly, this change allowed Smith to obtain employment and postgraduate education data at multiple points in time postgraduation: at 2, 5, and 10 years out. We thought it was important to contextualize our students' "first destinations" with information about how their careers developed and matured, providing better context for the long-term benefits of a liberal education.

New Directions for Institutional Research • DOI: 10.1002/ir

One challenge in implementing the project was that we in IR were concerned about the use of survey response data to populate alumnae records, including records that could be used to solicit donations. We resolved this concern by creating a set of questions allowing alumnae to opt out of or into sharing specific data points (occupation, industry, employer, job title, graduate school and program name, degrees sought, expected graduation, degrees earned, etc.) with identifying information attached.

These data are used to update the college's administrative systems, but they are also harnessed for departmental reports. These reports provide details of graduates' current activities alongside survey data on outcomes our faculty care about, but that are not as simple as first destinations. These include questions about alumnae ratings of their jobs' contribution to making the world a better place, volunteerism, entrepreneurship, satisfaction with preparation for careers and graduate school, work–life balance, and self-assessment of capacities.

We encourage faculty to give particular attention to postgraduate reflections on the capacities they developed as undergraduates. Unlike current students, whose ability to evaluate their own prowess in various areas is in some question (Pike, 1996), once a student graduates she is reflecting back on postgraduate experiences and the extent to which the undergraduate education prepared her for those experiences.

In addition to providing feedback at the departmental level, the ongoing survey provides an important data source that enables the ongoing institutional discussion of the outcomes of the liberal arts. We are able to track career growth and monitor how alumnae lifecycles have changed over the years. Contextualizing short-term outcomes with long-term ones is critical: although 73% of Smith alumnae held entry-level jobs at 2 years out, more than half of those 20 years out held positions at the senior or executive level.

Hampshire College: Appreciative Inquiry With "Thrivers"

Hampshire College began its current inquiry into student outcomes in the liberal arts when a trustee endowed a research program to understand how the Hampshire experience contributes to student outcomes. In a microcosm of the national debate, this trustee had been challenged by a colleague to provide evidence that the claims he made about Hampshire alumni were directly related to their undergraduate experiences at the college.

Hampshire is a liberal arts college that takes an unconventional, inquiry-based approach to student learning. Instead of offering majors, Hampshire students design their own courses of study culminating in a major project in the final year. Student experiences typically involve close faculty mentorship, experiential learning, and extensive interdisciplinary study. Hampshire was founded in 1970 as the fifth member of the Five College Consortium with Amherst College, Smith College, Mount Holyoke

NEW DIRECTIONS FOR INSTITUTIONAL RESEARCH • DOI: 10.1002/ir

College, and UMass Amherst, which expand the college's academic offerings through cross-registration (Hampshire College, 2016.

In one study begun in December 2013, in order to explore the question of outcomes, a research team comprised of the assessment director and IR director began with exploratory interviews on students they identified as "thriving" while at Hampshire. These students were interviewed during their time at Hampshire to explore their choice to enroll at Hampshire and their experiences there. In 2014, the interview pool was expanded to explore the effects of a Hampshire education further. In 2015, a subset of 25 of these same students were interviewed at 1 year out.

Wenk (2016) was able to use resources from the project endowment to hire a research associate to conduct and analyze qualitative interviews (those mentioned here as well as the development and implementation of a new longitudinal study beginning in students' first year). In the one-year-out interviews, alumni were asked about their employment and graduate school experiences and plans, but the interview went beyond these basic descriptors and asked students to reflect on how their Hampshire experiences affected their lives after graduation, including the content, skills, and abilities they learned at Hampshire.

Although data analysis is still in progress, Wenk (2016) reports that themes are already emerging from the research. Some alumni connected their Hampshire experience to a sense of balance and connection between work and life. Alumni saw their peers balancing separate jobs and personal lives, but many Hampshire alumni reported a sense of seamlessness to their lives, in which their working lives were deeply connected to their individual identities.

Wenk (2016) connects this outcome with Hampshire's curriculum, which is structured around students designing their own courses of study. Similarly, Hampshire alumni noted success in networking and finding mentorship, having a sense of purpose in their work, and the importance of social justice work in their postgraduate lives. When Wenk (2016) and colleagues reflect on these findings, they note direct connections to Hampshire's innovative liberal arts curriculum.

Although employment, entrepreneurship, and earnings are an obvious part of Hampshire's postgraduate outcomes assessment, Wenk (2016) stresses the value of qualitative research in understanding liberal arts outcomes that are less narrowly defined:

> Our whole assessment program for program improvement is based on qualitative research; interviews are central. This work came from a place of appreciative inquiry, what matters to students, what is happening when it's going well and how can we do more of that? That kind of data that feels contextually valid, the stories make sense, we see it every day. It also is fine grained enough in detail that you know what to do about it. If you have rubric data on x number of students do y, it doesn't tell you who is doing well or why. This

feels like what assessment ought to be. Thinking about goals for students, collecting data that tells us how they're doing. Data has to be rich enough to help take appropriate action.

Wenk (2016) advises institutional researchers who want to explore the deeper outcomes of liberal arts education to focus on qualitative methods that can allow stakeholders to explore student experiences in depth and to connect findings to the institution's mission in a meaningful way. The importance of assembling research teams that go beyond IR and assessment, particularly at the analytic stage, is also stressed. Wenk (2016) advises, "Share data across campus, make sure that anything we're doing is looked at with an eye to what we're learning from the qualitative research. We're always triangulating and confirming."

Carleton College: Leveraging an Alumni Data Warehouse to Connect Liberal Arts to Careers

Jim Fergerson at Carleton College was set on the path to developing a robust assessment of liberal arts outcomes by the president and board: the very first goal of the college's strategic plan focuses on outcomes, committing the college to "prepare students more robustly for fulfilling post-graduation lives and careers." The strategic plan also committed the institution to ongoing reporting of metrics related to its goals. This provided both a challenge to IR and an opportunity to leverage cross-campus collaboration to develop robust and detailed reporting on alumni outcomes.

Located in Northfield, Minnesota, Carleton College is a liberal arts college with an annual student enrollment of about 2,000 undergraduates. A highly selective residential college, it attracts students from across the United States and internationally, offering 33 majors along with several interdisciplinary programs. Carleton meets full financial need for all admitted students. Four out of five Carleton alums go on to graduate programs, and the college ranks highly among baccalaureate institutions in its production of academic doctorates (Carleton College, 2016).

IR worked closely with information technology, the career center, development, and others to make data collected and stored in disparate locations across the college available for meaningful, analytic reporting. IR was instrumental in changing the terms of the conversation about postgraduate employment. When the question was first formulated, it followed national norms, focusing on activities 1 year out of college. Through discussions with stakeholders, Fergerson (2015) was able to expand the time frame for reporting, collecting data from alumni over 25 years of graduating classes.

Working with a core recordkeeping system for tracking alumni that was primarily designed for communication and fundraising, Fergerson (2015) and his colleagues curated institutional records and combined them with survey data and external metrics to create a suite of reports that would provide students, advisors, alumni, and other stakeholders with detailed information about the careers and continuing education of graduates from each major. In addition to the data warehouse, Carleton uses data from the NSF Survey of Earned Doctorates to support claims about PhD production, and tracks medical school and law school admissions.

These reports included an interactive tool allowing students to explore the career trajectories of majors, demonstrating visually the flexibility of a liberal arts degree, along with department-specific reports, allowing the career center, advisors, and students to explore the career paths of alumni who majored in each discipline. These detailed reports provided foundational data for Carleton's strategic commitment to connecting the liberal arts with employment through specific, data-driven information about the pathways alumni have taken using their Carleton degrees.

Since assembling this data set, it has served Carleton well for a range of institutional questions. Fergerson (2015) says he has used it to respond to queries from around campus, including supporting department and program reviews and research proposals, answering questions about low-income/first-generation student outcomes, gender differences among STEM graduates, connections between internships and subsequent employment, and global connections and experiences. Several of these outcomes are incorporated into metrics that are shared regularly with senior staff and trustees.

Combining institutional records with survey data presented challenges that went beyond the political and the technical: Alumni surveys had traditionally been confidential, but now there was a reason to share the data across campus. Like Smith, Carleton revised its survey consent language to allow key employment and graduate school data to be used to update institutional data sets. Fergerson (2015) realized that alumni assumed data sharing despite confidentiality language: "we found that many seniors or alumni didn't update their alumni directory record when requested, because 'we already told you that on the survey.'"

The process of combining the various sources and then creating a repeatable, manageable process to report on student outcomes by department was a substantial one, requiring significant support from information technology and alumni relations. Developing consensus definitions and reporting strategies was an important part in Fergerson's ability to harness these disparate resources. He advises colleagues to "assemble a working team from several offices (IR, Alumni, Central Records, Career Center, Deans, Web staff, IT) to discuss and plan ahead for any data or coding issues that may arise. We saved countless hours by spending some extra time discussing what standard career reporting categories we would use, and how they would be stored in the alumni database" (Fergerson, 2015).

Alumni Reflections at Trinity College

Rachael Barlow of Trinity College seized an opportunity to collect deeper information about the effect of the liberal arts on alumni careers when she consulted to a committee charged with updating alumni profile information. Through this broadly distributed profile query, Trinity included a set of qualitative research questions asking alumni to reflect on how the liberal arts have shaped their careers.

Trinity College is a private, nonsectarian liberal arts college located in Hartford, Connecticut. With 2,200 undergraduate students, Trinity offers 39 majors, including an ABET-accredited engineering program. Trinity is known for its innovative Center for Urban and Global studies and its strong Division III athletics programs. More than half of Trinity students study abroad or away during their Trinity careers (Trinity College, 2016).

The project grew out of a faculty committee that was charged with improving Trinity's institutional data about alumni employment and careers. Trinity was interested in keeping better track of alumni, but faculty also saw the survey as an opportunity to provide specific information to current students about how alumni had translated majors into careers. This information would be available to faculty and administrators for alumni engagement, advising, and networking for current students seeking internships and jobs. Many faculty felt ill-equipped to counsel students on transitioning from liberal arts majors to careers, and this project provided an opportunity to make that link explicit through the lives of alumni.

Barlow (2016) points out what she calls an "interesting tension between what you majored in and what a liberal arts college does and then what do you do as an alum." Barlow (2016) said the committee saw the opportunity to expand the concept of connecting majors to careers to one where they could ask students to reflect more broadly: "If you major in English, it's not necessarily useful to only talk to English alumni. This is a liberal arts college; who cares what the major was? Let's talk about something bigger that has more to do with the more general liberal arts experience than any specific major."

As a consultant to the committee, Barlow (2016) saw her role as a facilitator, helping faculty achieve consensus on research decisions and implementing the survey. Ultimately, the committee fielded a survey that included a list of six qualitative questions that supplemented the standard employment update. These included questions about how the liberal arts education has helped in alumni careers, aspects of the Trinity experience that contributed to advancing career goals, advice to current students interested in preparing for their current field, and what they think the biggest misconception about their field is.

Barlow (2016) reports that far from being a burden, the additional questions provided incentive to respond to the survey. "[Alumni] were really happy to talk about those things and be asked about those things and it made the side project of gathering the employment data more palatable. So it wasn't just about what job you got, but giving them the option to talk about what a liberal arts education meant to them." The most unusual question on the list, which asked about alumni views of the biggest misconception in their fields, turned out to be one of the most fruitful. "As we talk about how we're educating our students for this postgraduate world that most of us don't actually know anything about—I think that's useful because I suspect faculty themselves have a lot of the same misperceptions about some of those fields that they're advising students to go into" (Barlow, 2016).

Conclusion

Clearly, the project of supplying evidence to support the value of a liberal arts education is not a simple one. The case studies presented above provide a small sampling of the ways institutional researchers are approaching this project.

For many institutions, the work of documenting the employment and graduate school outcomes of graduates is a data integration and organizational challenge. In these situations, IR practitioners have been successful brokers and aggregators, leveraging relationships and technical skills to develop data sources that are reliable and meet multiple campus needs. Though the case studies illustrate that this can be a significant undertaking, resources and reports that illustrate connections between future careers and majors in the liberal arts are widely valued, garnering positive receptions from admission, academic advising, and career services among others.

Some institutions go beyond documenting outcomes to exploring the mission-driven value of a liberal arts education. Sometimes these studies are resource-intensive qualitative explorations, and sometimes institutional researchers take the opportunity to explore these larger issues when requesting postgraduate outcomes data on employment and education. By necessity, this work is exploratory for most campuses, but institutional researchers can help to inform campus conversations about connecting the liberal arts with employment by collecting student feedback and identifying key themes.

As mentioned in chapter 1 of this issue, the AAC&U defines the goal of liberal education to prepare students to live responsible and productive lives, and the LEAP initiative provides a framework for examining these outcomes. The case studies presented here reflect the spirit of the LEAP initiative by providing examples of how institutions can use collaborative and data-driven approaches to better understand and document the connection between their graduates' education and future endeavors beyond first-destination outcomes.

In addition, AAC&U's LEAP initiative can offer a valuable resource for institutional researchers interested in enhancing outcomes assessment to provide a framework for connecting mission-driven liberal arts learning to success in future employment. AAC&U has conducted employer surveys that largely validate the importance of institutional learning outcomes like oral and written communication, ability to work in teams, ethical decision-making, critical thinking skills, and the ability to apply knowledge to real-world situations (Hart Research, 2015, p. 4). Institutional researchers may find ways to use LEAP and associated research to help institutions make explicit connections between liberal arts outcomes and preparation for career success.

As always, qualitative and quantitative approaches appeal to different audiences to different extents, and institutional researchers must be sensitive to these stakeholder preferences and to the degree of development of the campus conversation about liberal arts outcomes. It is clear that IR practitioners are uniquely positioned to foster and inform these discussions, both on campus and in the public debate.

References

American Association of Colleges and Universities (AAC&U). (2014). *An introduction to LEAP*. Washington, DC: AAC&U.

Barlow, R. (2016, 1 14). Liberal arts case studies. (C. Rowen, Interviewer)

Carleton College (2016). About Carleton. Retrieved January 2016 from https://apps .carleton.edu/about/

Fergerson, J. (2015). Liberal arts case studies. (C. Rowen, Interviewer)

Finley, A. (2012). *Making progress? What we know about the achievement of liberal education outcomes*. Washington, DC: AAC&U.

Goudreau, J. (2012). The 10 worst college majors. *Forbes*. Retrieved from http://www .forbes.com/sites/jennagoudreau/2012/10/11/the-10-worst-college-majors/#4b7bfc41 53c9

Hampshire College. (2016). Discover Hampshire. Retrieved January 2016 from https:// www.hampshire.edu/discover-hampshire/discover-hampshire-college

Hart Research Associates. (2015). *Falling Short? College Learning and Career Success*. Washington, DC: AAC&U. Retrieved from https://www.aacu.org/sites/default/files /files/LEAP/2015employerstudentsurvey.pdf

Kessler, G. A. (2015). Fact checking the fourth round of GOP debates. *The Washington Post*. Retrieved from https://www.washingtonpost.com/news/fact-checker/wp /2015/11/11/fact-checking-the-fourth-round-of-gop-debates/

PayScale. (2016). *PayScale college ROI*. Retrieved from http://www.payscale.com /college-roi

Pike, G. R. (1996). Limitations of using students' self-reports of academic development as proxies for traditional achievement measures. *Research in Higher Education*. Retrieved from http://www.jstor.org/stable/40196212

Smith College. (2016). About Smith. Retrieved January 2016 from http://www.smith.edu /about-smith

Trinity College. (2016). About Trinity. Retrieved January 2016 from http://www .trincoll.edu/abouttrinity/Pages/default.aspx

Wenk, L. (2016). Liberal arts case studies. (C. Rowen, Interviewer)

CATE ROWEN *is the executive director of institutional research at Smith College in Northampton, Massachusetts.*

NEW DIRECTIONS FOR INSTITUTIONAL RESEARCH • DOI: 10.1002/ir

5

Postgraduation outcomes for community college students are complex. In addition to traditional job placement and earnings information, transferring to a 4-year institution is a positive first-destination outcome. Furthermore, community college students may have education and career goals that do not include earning a degree. Community college measures of success, two case studies, and how community colleges use outcomes data will be discussed.

Community Colleges: Preparing Students for Diverse Careers

Lou A. Guthrie

Students, parents, college administration, and policy makers are demanding more data on former students' first-destination outcomes. The labor-market outcomes for community college students usually include job placement, percentages, and average earnings, very similar to the measures used by 4-year institutions. However, instead of looking at graduate/professional school enrollment as an outcome, community colleges consider students transferring to a 4-year institution as a positive first-destination outcome. Community colleges also have the confounding factor of awarding certificates in addition to awarding associate degrees. Unlike the Associate in Arts or Associate in Science degrees, certificate programs can be any number of credit hours which makes job placement and earnings outcomes for students completing them difficult to track and also difficult to compare.

Another issue that affects community colleges more than 4-year colleges and universities is the number of students who attend community college to only take one or two career or technical courses. These "skills builders" are typically considered "noncompleters" and have not been counted as a success for community colleges. Thus, their increased income has not been included in labor-market outcomes data. The postgraduation outcomes for community college students are complex and exceptionally difficult to collect and report, but they are becoming more readily available.

The term "community college" generally refers to not-for-profit institutions regionally accredited to award Associate in Arts (AA) or Associate in Science (AS) degrees. The 2015 Carnegie Classification of Institutions in Higher Education (http://carnegieclassifications.iu.edu/) "Associate's Colleges" indicates there are 1,113 colleges making up 24% of postsecondary

New Directions for Institutional Research, no. 169 © 2016 Wiley Periodicals, Inc.
Published online in Wiley Online Library (wileyonlinelibrary.com) • DOI: 10.1002/ir.20170

institutions in the United States. These institutions had 32% of the fall 2014 total enrollment in higher education (6,524,819 students). Carnegie classifies community colleges based on their program focus and their size. Figure 5.1 shows that for program focus, community colleges are split three ways. Thirty-four percent of the colleges are classified as high transfer institutions that typically offer programs with credits that are accepted by 4-year institutions based on articulation agreements or in some states, decreed by legislation. An additional 35% of the colleges are classified as high vocational and technical colleges, meaning they offer education that prepares people to work in a trade, in a craft, or as a technician, and are also referred to as career education or technical education.

Figure 5.2 shows how Carnegie splits community colleges down by size. Although the number of large and very large community colleges are considerably less, they enroll a relatively higher proportion of the students. The Carnegie report notes that the majority of community colleges enroll large proportions of part-time students, which is the reverse of the situation at 4-year institutions.

Community colleges also have a higher proportion of nontraditional students than 4-year institutions. The Lumina Foundation calls them "21st century students" and the National Center for Education Statistics (1996) has identified the following seven characteristics associated with these students:

- Do not immediately continue education after graduation from high school
- Attend college only part time
- Work full time (35 hours or more per week)
- Are financially independent
- Have children or dependents other than their spouse
- Are a single parent
- Have a GED, not a high school diploma

According to Cohen, Brawer, and Kisker (2016), "Unlike full-time students at residential, four-year universities, whose lives may revolve around classes, peers and social events, community college students often struggle to fit required courses, tutoring and other educational activities into schedules constrained by part- or full-time jobs, family commitments, child-rearing responsibilities, long commutes, or other obligations." Adding open-access mandates or open-door policies with less academically-prepared students that take considerably longer to complete adds another layer of complexity to the measurement of employment metrics.

Diverse institutions, nontraditional students, many of which are already employed, transfer-based programs, and longer enrollment time frames all create barriers to collecting and reporting meaningful job placement rates and earnings of community college students. Community

Figure 5.1. Associate's Level Colleges and Statistics on Undergraduate Instructional Program Focus (Carnegie Classification of Institutions of Higher Education, 2015)

Associate's Colleges - Undergraduate Instructional Program Focus

	Institutions		Fall 2014 Enrollment	
	N	%	N	%
High Transfer	377	34%	3,276,783	50%
Mixed Transfer/Vocational & Technical	342	31%	2,238,359	34%
High Vocational & Technical	394	35%	1,009,677	15%
Grand Total	1,113		6,524,819	

Note: The data above reflect all community colleges, including a small representation of private institutions, both nonprofit and for profit.

Figure 5.2. Size Categories of Students at 2-Year Institutions (Carnegie Classification of Institutions of Higher Education, 2015)

Size Categories* at Two-Year Institutions

	Institutions		Fall 2014 Enrollment	
	N	%	N	%
Very Small (<500)	531	34%	152,431	2%
Small (500-1,999)	470	30%	768,066	11%
Medium (2,000-4,999)	329	21%	1,811,740	27%
Large (5,000-9,999)	174	11%	2,057,389	31%
Very Large (10,000+)	75	5%	1,947,061	29%
Grand Total	1,579		6,736,687	

Note: The data above reflect all community colleges, including a small representation of private institutions, both nonprofit and for profit.

college institutional research offices recognize the challenging conditions and address these issues in a variety of ways.

Community College Measures of Success

Before you can begin to look at the labor-market outcomes of community college students, you need first to determine what constitutes completion. Unlike 4-year institutions, it is widely recognized that official graduation rates (e.g., U.S. Department of Education, http://www.ed.gov/) are an inadequate measure for community colleges. Graduation rates look only at a

New Directions for Institutional Research • DOI: 10.1002/ir

small subset of community college students, as they typically refer to students that enroll in the fall, are first-time students, attend college full-time, and are degree-seeking. Graduation rates are also be examined based on a time frame allowed for completion. Community colleges typically look at on-time rates (2 years), 3-year or 150% of normal time, and 6-year graduation rates. These varying time-frames help take into consideration the plethora of part-time students at community colleges.

The first-time student variable complicates the graduation rate picture. For example, institutional research offices typically break out students by those that are getting their associate's degree that have no prior certifications or college experience (transfer-ins). Students that transfer-in from other institutions, those that already have one AA or AS degree, or have earned other postsecondary credentials, such as a certificate or license, are tracked separately, as are students that indicate they are not seeking a specific degree or certificate. Thus even the basic measure of graduation rates do not tell the full picture of success for community colleges.

In April 2010, the American Association of Community Colleges (AACC), the League for Innovation in the Community College, Association of Community College Trustees, the National Institute for Staff and Organizational Development, Phi theta Kappa, and the Center for Community College Student Engagement signed a commitment to produce 50% more students with degrees and certificates by 2020. This commitment was an impetus for community colleges to start to look at not just graduation rates, but look at the actual number of degrees and certificates that they award.

Certificates

Transfers, Swirling, and Double-Dipping.   Because many community college students attend with the express purpose of transferring to a 4-year institution, transfer rates are an important component of success. Most community colleges track their transfers with the National Student Clearinghouse. Examining how well their students do, the grades they receive, and whether they get a degree at a 4-year institution are additional measures of success that community colleges track, although comparable metrics with clear definitions are not used across the board. Jenkins and Fink (2016) have developed a common set of three metrics for measuring the effectiveness of 2-year institutions in regards to their success of preparing and enabling their students to transfer to 4-year institutions and attain a degree: (a) transfer-out rate, (b) transfer-with-award rate, and (c) transfer-out bachelor's completion rates. The National Community College Benchmark Project (NCCBP) (https://nccbp.org) currently measures transfer-out rates and the transfer-with-award rates. To check on the success of students after they transfer, the NCCBP measures cumulative first-year GPA (at a 4-year institution), total first-year credit hours, and the persistence of transfer students. However, the transfer-out bachelor's completion rates have been very difficult for community college institutional researchers to track and are not included in the NCCBP. The National Student Clearinghouse has this information, but to access it, you must do an individual student lookup via their Web site, which is very time-consuming.

Transfer rates are getting more complicated as more students attend multiple colleges, take on-line courses from colleges other than their "main" institution, and generally "swirl" throughout higher education. The Clearinghouse has a reverse transfer program that allows colleges to send student course and grade information to any 2-year institution from which a student has transferred. This allows the 2-year institution to award an associate degree once students are eligible, even if some of their coursework is completed after they transfer out of the 2-year institution. The reverse-transfer concept allows community colleges to increase their completion rates, giving them credit for students who move on to other institutions and continue their education.

Post–Community College Labor-Market Outcomes.   Labor-market outcomes are used by students to help make the choice of where to go to college and in choosing a major. These outcomes are also critical to policymakers, with earnings data included in the "College Scorecard" and on many state consumer information Web sites. In addition, seven states have included some form of labor outcomes in their performance funding models. The College Scorecard (https://collegescorecard.ed.gov/) is not an effective tool for students looking to choose a community college. The graduation rates listed do not include certificates or transfers and thus present an incomplete picture of the success rates for 2-year colleges. These same flaws make the College Scorecard an ineffective tool for policymakers.

By far, the most-used key performance metric related to outcomes for community college students is the percent of these graduates that are employed. This is usually divided into students that are employed in their area of study and those employed in another business or industry category. The Bureau of Labor Statistics looks at unemployment rates and earnings based on educational attainment. In 2014, the unemployment rate for individuals with an associate's degree was 4.5%, whereas the rates for those with some college or only a high school diploma were 6%. Individuals with an associate's degree also earned $51 more per week than people with some college, but no degree. They earned $124 more per week than high school graduates.

College Outcomes Data

Completers Survey.   The most common and sometimes the only available method to collect job placement and earnings data is from a completer survey. Typically, all students who completed a degree or a certificate during the academic year are emailed a survey approximately 6 months after graduation. Some colleges use mailed surveys for the process but as printing and mailing costs have increased more community colleges are opting to do the first round of data collection via e-mail.

After giving 2–3 weeks for the former students to respond to the e-mail survey, most colleges send out a second round of data-collection surveys by mail. The second round would normally include students who did not have valid e-mail addresses, plus all those who did not respond to the e-mail survey.

To increase their response rates, some colleges take one more step by attempting to contact their former students via telephone. Even after applying all of these methods, many community colleges do not get the response rates they would like. Typical response rates are 20–22%. Research has been conducted to determine if the survey mode impacts the return rate. Results have been mixed with some research showing on-line response rates being higher than other modes of (mail and telephone) and other research concluding the opposite.

It should be noted that many researchers do not think self-reported salary information is totally accurate. This is leading to a movement to encourage states' departments of labor to work with their community colleges to supply data in an effort to make outcomes data on job placements and salaries more accurate. In some states, their department of revenue also provides salary and job placement data to contribute to state data banks.

Case Studies

As community colleges both collect and use labor-market outcomes data in a variety of ways, two case studies are provided to highlight some of the methods and uses. Johnson County Community College will be used to show how completer surveys are conducted and reported. Information about Monroe Community College's Accelerated Precision Tooling Certificate (APTC) program will be shared to illustrate how technical programs use labor-market intelligence to help design programs and to report outcome results for those programs.

Johnson County Community College, Kansas. Johnson County Community College (JCCC) in Overland Park, Kansas, does an annual follow-up survey of program completers and prepares an annual report of the results (see http://www.jccc.edu/about/leadership-governance /administration/institutional-research/index.html).

The JCCC survey looks at students who were awarded associate's degrees and certificates. The survey goes beyond looking at just employment rates and wages. Students are asked if they have achieved their educational objectives and if they are currently enrolled in higher education. They are asked to indicate if they have taken a state licensing exam or industry certificate exam since leaving the college.

In terms of employment, the program completers are asked if they are employed in a field related to their program of study, employed in an unrelated field, are in the military full-time, or are working at an apprenticeship. The unemployed are asked if they are looking for work or not in the labor force.

Johnson County Community College also includes results from an employer survey in their completers report. The respondents to the survey who indicated they were employed in a field related to their area of study were asked to identify their employer. Questionnaires were then sent to the employers asking them to evaluate the overall job preparation of the JCCC program completers. Much of the information collected in the survey appears at the program level.

Monroe Community College, New York.   Todd Oldham, Vice President, Economic Development and Innovative Workforce Services at Monroe Community College (MCC) in Rochester, New York, uses labor-market intelligence extensively, both in the design and evaluation of programs. The MCC Accelerated Precision Tooling Certificate Program is a strategic initiative designed and executed in response to skills gaps in the advanced manufacturing industry in the Finger Lakes Region. It was created as an innovative approach to address a large deficit in the supply of qualified technician based workers documented though MCC's labor-market intelligence analyses (see Measuring Middle-Skills Occupational Gaps within the Finger Lakes Regional Economy, http://www.workforceforward.com/SkillsGap). This report measures the supply of workers being created through the region's education system against the estimated labor demand for occupations aligned to their respective programs. The analysis includes a close look at wages relative to the local self-sufficiency standard.

The MCC Accelerated Precision Tooling Certificate program is designed to prepare students for employment in the advanced manufacturing industry in a shorter period of time compared to traditionally taught programs. A unique feature of the program is active job placement, which is provided by MCC's partner, the Rochester Technology & Manufacturing Association (RTM). Upon completion of the program, students are placed in an entry-level machining-related position in a local manufacturing company. The accelerated program directly addresses the needs of employers within the advanced manufacturing industry sector in the Greater Rochester Area and Finger Lakes Region by measurably increasing the number of skilled graduates in the local economy.

MCC's Economic Development and Innovative Workforce Services Division (EDIWS) has conducted four Accelerated Precision Tooling Certificate cohorts since its inception in May 2013. On average, the cohorts have achieved a 75–80% completion rate and an average 90% job placement rate. This represents a significantly higher completion rate compared to the 33% completion rate for the first-time, full-time students enrolled in the traditionally taught certificate program completing within 3 years' time.

NEW DIRECTIONS FOR INSTITUTIONAL RESEARCH • DOI: 10.1002/ir

MCC worked with Burning Glass Technologies (http://burning-glass .com/higher-education/) and their Labor Insight program to incorporate real-time labor-market information into their strategic planning for programs. Burning Glass mines job postings and the data can be used by college administration to identify opportunities for new or expanded programs and to stay in touch with the specific skills, credentials and locations of job markets for their programs. There are a number of other big data subscription services that provide labor-market data to colleges. In addition to Burning Glass, MCC also partners closely with Emsi in utilizing both their Analyst and Career Coach programs (http://www.economicmodeling.com).

Gainful Employment

The Student-Right-To-Know and Campus Security Act of 1990 requires all colleges and universities participating in the Federal Student Aid Program to disclose basic institution information, graduation rates, and information on students receiving athletically related student aid, campus security policies, and campus crime statistics. Pursuant to 20 USCS Section 1092, each eligible institution must provide the following information:

- Cost of attending the institution, including (1) tuition and fees, (2) books and supplies, (3) estimates of typical student room and board cost or typical commuting costs, and (4) any additional costs that the program which the student is enrolled or expresses a specific interest in;
- The completion or graduation rates of certificate-or degree-seeking, full-time, undergraduate students entering such institution.

In addition, a specific form is required for each gainful employment program of study at the college. Figure 5.3 shows an example of one of these forms.

The Kansas Training Information Program (K-TIP) also prepares a report on job-market outcomes for all Kansas approved postsecondary career technical education programs (http://www.kansasregents.org/). The information is compiled from data submitted to the Kansas Board of Regents by individual institutions. The data submitted by the Kansas colleges are supplemented with data provided by the Kansas Department of Labor. However, the information obtained from the Kansas Department of Labor on program completers is not shared with the individual community colleges.

Community Colleges Use Their Outcomes Data

Community college placement rates and earnings are not as visible or publicized as much as other measures of success. For example, Community College Review (http://www.communitycollegereview.com/) is a Web site designed to give potential students and their parents information

New Directions for Institutional Research • DOI: 10.1002/ir

Figure 5.3. Example of Student's Right to Know Information

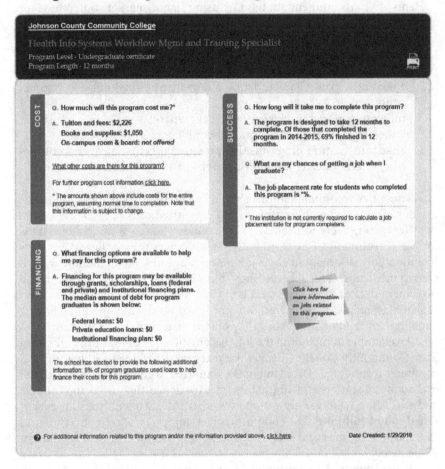

about community colleges; for example, student-to-teacher ratios, minority enrollment and a diversity score, and tuition and fees information can be found. Interestingly enough, completion and transfer rates or job placement rates or earnings are not provided. The College Scorecard, the U.S. Department of Education's Web site for consumers to compare colleges, on the other hand, has a section titled, "Earnings after School." This section reports the percentage of students who attended the school who earned, on average, more than those with only a high school diploma. Also reported is the salary after attending, compared with the national average. This salary information is institution-wide, not by program.

State Performance or Outcomes-Based Funding. Currently, 30 states have outcome-based funding models and most of the models center on graduation rates and other measures of college success. Only seven include job placement and earnings metrics. Anna Cielinski (2015) presents five recommendations for using labor-market outcomes for accountability:

1. Use earnings/employment data by program of study, not institution-wide.
2. Take participant characteristics and/or institutional mission into account.
3. Index to regional wage/economic benchmarks.
4. Disaggregate completers from noncompleters.
5. Take into account programs that provide skills that meet community/labor-market needs, even if these jobs have lower average earnings.

These five recommendations should be taken into consideration in the use of earnings and employment data in any situation.

Recruiting New Students.   One common usage of outcomes data is for the recruitment of new students. Many community college Web sites include information about their job placement rates. Some include overall employment rates and job earnings, but the most common usage of job placement data and earnings data is at the program level. This information is shared to help students select a major based on the likelihood of getting a job in their field of study after they obtain their degree or certificate.

An example of including the job placement data comes from Pellissippi State Community College (http://www.pstcc.edu/). "The BCT [business and computer technology] Department is committed to giving students both the classroom education and the hands-on experience they need to compete and excel in a wide variety of fields. And the department does an exceptional job of fulfilling that commitment: it enjoys an excellent reputation in the Knoxville area and has a long-term job placement rate of more than 90 percent."

Recruitment of Faculty and Staff.   Another usage of these data is in the recruitment of faculty and staff. For example, one college that is in the midst of a presidential search included this information in their candidate's criterion document (http://www.statetechmo.edu/):

> The State Technical College of Missouri, a nationally ranked public two-year technical college, is seeking a president . . . The State Technical College has a statewide mission to prepare students for profitable employment and a life of learning. The more than 1,200 current students in associate of applied science degree and certificate programs come from over eighty percent of the counties in Missouri to attend. The Technical College also provides short-term occupational training and prides itself in its close relationship with employers. The graduate placement rate is ninety-five percent. It is a key contributor to the state and its regional workforce needs and is proud of its responsiveness to those needs.

NEW DIRECTIONS FOR INSTITUTIONAL RESEARCH • DOI: 10.1002/ir

Program Review and To Provide information to Administration and Boards. Community colleges also use job placement and earnings data for program review and evaluation. When examining the cost and effectiveness of programs, labor-market outcomes usually play a large role. Programs that have low placement rates are more likely to be eliminated. Earnings data may not be as useful in program review because they do not take into account the need in the community for the program skills or the benefit to society that are directly associated with jobs that have lower salaries.

Conclusion

Community colleges today are mainly focused on measures of successful completion: degrees and certificates granted and transfer rates. Outcomes data are primarily short-term economic information, such as placement rates and first-year salaries. These data are mainly used to show students the economic value of various certificates or degree programs or to illustrate meeting the community's economic development needs for various programs of study.

The way community colleges measure successful outcomes is in a state of flux. Changes are being made rapidly and some states, notably California (http://datamart.cccco.edu/) and Texas (http://www.txhighereddata.org/ and College Measures http://www.collegemeasures.org/) are making great strides in measuring outcomes. Recently California incorporated ways to measure the impact a few credits, but no degree or certification, had on the wages of these noncompleters. They are also looking at job promotions for this group, which they have labeled "skills builders," and these measures will be added to the state's publicly available scorecard assessment of the performance of their 113 community colleges. This measure will likely spread throughout the country, offering a way to measure outcomes for a group of students that have been missing from the outcomes picture.

In the future, outcomes data may be less focused on the economic value of a postsecondary education and more attention will likely be paid to the social capital value of a postsecondary education, both at the public and personal levels. The Bill and Melinda Gates Foundation supported a project, Post-Collegiate Outcomes Framework and Toolkit (http://www.aacc.nche.edu/AboutCC/), to provide a more comprehensive discussion on the measures that help determine the value of a college education. This framework, a result of collaborations with the American Association of Community Colleges (AACC), the American Association of State Colleges and Universities (AASCU), and the Association of Public and Land-grant Universities (APLU), attempts to answer the question, "What is the value of a college education?"

The Gallup-Purdue Index (http://www.gallup.com) is another initiative being used to measure the impact of a college education. Purdue University,

Gallup, and the Lumina Foundation released the inaugural Gallup-Purdue Index in May 2014, "Great Jobs, Great Lives." It is the largest representative study of college graduates in U.S. history and the initiative aims to create a national movement toward a new set of outcomes measures that go beyond the traditional financial outcomes associated with a college degree or certificate.

With these new initiatives, community colleges will start to look beyond labor-market outcomes for their programs and focus on the long-term impact of an associate's degree or a certificate. They will look at the overall well-being, health, happiness, community, and social benefits a community college education can provide.

References

Carnegie Classification of Institutions of Higher Education. (2015). *Update facts & figures*. Bloomington, IN: Center for Postsecondary Research, Indiana University School of Education.

Cielinski, A. (2015, October). *Using post-college labor market outcomes: policy challenges and choices*. Washington, DC: Center for Postsecondary and Economic Success.

Cohen, A. M., Brawer, F. B., & Kisker, C. B. (2016, January). *The American community college, 2014*. San Francisco, CA: Jossey-Bass.

Jenkins, D., & Fink, J. (2016, January). *Tracking transfer*. New York, NY: Community College Research Center.

National Center for Education Statistics. (1996, November). *Nontraditional undergraduates/definitions and data*. Retrieved from http://nces.ed.gov/

LOU A. GUTHRIE *is the director of the National Higher Education Benchmarking Institute located at Johnson County Community College in Overland Park, Kansas.*

NEW DIRECTIONS FOR INSTITUTIONAL RESEARCH • DOI: 10.1002/ir

This chapter will address the importance of intercampus involvement in reporting of gainful employment student-level data that will be used in the calculation of gainful employment metrics by the U.S. Department of Education. The authors will discuss why building relationships within the institution is critical for effective gainful employment reporting.

6

Leading Gainful Employment Metric Reporting

Kristina Powers, Derek MacPherson

Assessment of postgraduate outcomes has substantially evolved over the last 5 years to focus on obtaining employment as well as job earnings as interested groups, such as prospective students, their parents, taxpayers, and legislators, have attempted to compare return on investment among higher education institutions. Throughout all chapters of this volume, authors have described the difficulties with measuring postgraduate outcomes, including satisfaction, employment, and earnings. Although there is no absolute, there are multiple methods and practices for conducting alumni surveys and reporting on the results. Because this is an evolving area, institutions have taken the liberty to develop methodologies that fit their institution, and perhaps create a methodology that will be seen and followed by other institutions as a best practice.

Although there is typically institutional freedom to collect and report postgraduate outcomes data for most items, such liberties do not exist for government reporting, where directions and definitions must be followed. One such example is the U.S. Department of Education's required reporting of gainful employment (GE) data for the calculation of GE metrics. Given that institutional researchers typically lead federal and state reporting (Henderson, 2016), it makes sense that their expertise and experience will be used whenever there is new and/or complex mandatory government reporting, which is the case with GE. This chapter will focus on the institutional data submission that is used in the U.S. Department of Education's calculation of GE metrics by program. Institutional research (IR) is the likely leader of the submission and/or is doing substantial portions of the data pull.

New Directions for Institutional Research, no. 169 © 2016 Wiley Periodicals, Inc.
Published online in Wiley Online Library (wileyonlinelibrary.com) • DOI: 10.1002/ir.20171

Brief Background of GE and GE Data Reporting

The term GE is a large umbrella that encompasses multiple elements. The federal GE regulations were first issued in 2011, but significant litigation caused the U.S. Department of Education to issue substantially revised GE regulations in 2014. The initial GE regulations from 2011 were documented and analyzed by several researchers, including Hentschke and Parry (2014), Serna (2014), and Xu (2014). However, for institutional researchers either new to the topic of GE or interested in strategies for making institutional changes in response to GE, Thompson Coburn (2014) proposed a methodology for estimating GE results.

Which Institutions Need to Report?   All institutions are potentially impacted, including public and private not-for-profit institutions. Even though many people may think of GE as a requirement for for-profit institutions, according to the federal regulation [FR 64890] (U.S. Department of Education, 2014), "GE programs include nearly all educational programs at for-profit institutions of higher education, as well as non-degree programs at public and private nonprofit institutions such as community colleges." (p. 2). More specifically, in addition to programs at for-profit institutions, GE applies to "public institutions and not-for-profit institutions, all Title IV eligible, non-degree programs are GE Programs except for: Programs of at least two years in length that are designed to be fully transferable to a bachelor's degree program; Preparatory coursework necessary for enrollment in an eligible program" (U.S. Department of Education, 2015, p. 8). The addition of public and not-for-profit programs and certificate programs was a significant change in the 2014 regulations.

Additionally, it is important for institutions that do not have a qualifying program, but are considering adding a new program, to know that gainful employment reporting and implications may result. As such, careful consideration should be given to include institutional researchers in feasibility studies for new programs so that GE considerations and estimates for passing the GE metrics are addressed in the curriculum development process. Addressing these considerations after program implementation can be challenging for the institution.

What Information Is Reported and When Is it Due?   The federal regulation [FR 64890] (U.S. Department of Education, 2014), provides the details regarding the data items required for submission. Additionally, the U.S. Department of Education has provided a number of resource guides, webinars, and documents that include additional details regarding file specifications and submission instructions. Resources can be found on the Information for Financial Aid Professionals (IFAP) iLibrary at https://ifap.ed.gov/ifap/iLibrary.jsp. Documents such as the NSLDS User Guide (National Student Loan Data System, 2015) and Gainful Employment Reporting to NSLDS Webinar (U.S. Department of Education, 2015) are critical resources for institutional researchers who are involved in GE.

NEW DIRECTIONS FOR INSTITUTIONAL RESEARCH • DOI: 10.1002/ir

The data report is due October 1 of each year. (The initial submission of GE reporting in 2015 was due on July 31 and included 6 years of data.) However, because the reporting period is July 1 to June 30, the data are available to be pulled any time after June 30 that would enable a complete data set. Most institutions need at least 45 days after June 30 (i.e., August 15) before extracting data to allow sufficient time for returning any title IV (R2T4) funds. An additional week or so may be needed for student information systems to update data prior to running reports.

In the best-case scenario, this means data are pulled by the IR/Information Technology (IT)/Business Intelligence (BI) team approximately August 15, leaving just 6 weeks for subject-matter experts to review and test the data. It is important that those individuals have sufficient time to review, provide feedback, IT/BI to make adjustments, and then test again. Because it is likely that 6 weeks is not enough time to complete this task, institutions should consider running draft reports. The data can be extracted even earlier and pretests of the logic model can be completed. This process will minimize the amount of work on the IR/IT/BI or subject-matter expert teams during short period of time.

What Are the Data Used For?   Once submitted, the U.S. Department of Education uses the data to engage in multiple phases. Each phase is only briefly described here as the purpose of this chapter is to on the data submission. Yet, it is always important to understand how data are going to be used prior to submitting reports.

Similarly, it is also important to distinguish between data reporting and disclosure reporting. Although this article focuses on the data reporting, the annual GE disclosures have different information that must be publicly displayed on each program's Web site, with the use of the Department of Education's (DOE) required template, by January 31 of each year. Additional details about the GE disclosures can be found at https://www.ifap.ed.gov/ea nnouncements/102315GEAnnounce65DisclosureTemplateforGEProg1415 .html and technical information about the GE disclosure template can be found at http://ope.ed.gov/GainfulEmployment/GEDT_Quick_Start_Guide _Internet_Explorer.pdf

GE Program Tracker List.   The GE Program Tracker list "allows institutions to view a list of GE programs that have been reported to NSLDS by institutional Gainful Employment reporting and/or COD" (National Student Loan Data System, 2015, p. 30). Institutions are expected to review the list for accuracy and provide a status update, if applicable. Because there is a list for each academic year, review takes place on an annual basis. More details are described in the GE User Guide. However, it is important to note that the GE User Guide is updated as new information becomes available. Therefore, obtaining the latest GE user guide is critical.

GE Completers List and Appeals.   With the use of the GE data that the institution submits, the DOE identifies the subset of records that meets the criteria for inclusion in the GE metrics. Institutions have an opportunity to review the list, which the DOE will use to obtain the earnings for students in each GE program (National Student Loan Data System, 2015). Institutions can submit an appeal, requesting to include additional students that were omitted or exclude students who were included that the institution believes should be omitted. The institution must provide evidence for the basis of their appeal. More details are described in the GE User Guide.

Calculation and Release of Metrics.   After obtaining earnings data from the Social Security Administration, the DOE calculates two metrics, the Annual Earnings Rate (AER) and the Discretionary Income Rate (DIR). The resulting calculation yields a category of fail, zone, or pass. A GE program must pass either the AER or the DIR, otherwise the institution must comply with additional regulations, which are outlined in Section 668.405 of the final regulations published in the Federal Register on October 31, 2014:

> Under the regulations, to pass the D/E (debt to earnings) rates measure, the GE program must have a discretionary income rate 2 less than or equal to 20% or an annual earnings rate 3 less than or equal to 8%. The regulations also establish a zone for GE programs that have a discretionary income rate greater than 20% and less than or equal to 30% or an annual earnings rate greater than 8% and less than or equal to 12%. GE programs with a discretionary income rate over 30% and an annual earnings rate over 12% will fail the D/E rates measure. Under the regulations, a GE program becomes ineligible for title IV, HEA program funds, if it fails the D/E rates measure for two out of three consecutive years, or has a combination of D/E rates that are in the zone or failing for four consecutive year (U.S. Department of Education, 2014, p. 3).

Value of Intercampus Relationships

Given the nature of IR work, which is largely data oriented (e.g., pulling, analyzing, and synthesizing data for external submission or internal use) many institutional researchers spend most of their time working independently. However, in order to use the data, it is paramount to have contextual understanding of the data as well as policies and procedures that influence them. For example, a technical analyst could pull data from the student information system and report that there are 15 students in the political science major.

Depending upon the parameters that the analyst selected, that response may be correct. However, when returning back to the requestor's question of "how many political science students do we currently have?" The analyst needs context in order to ensure the accuracy of the information, otherwise the analyst risks reporting an inaccurate number.

An example of context in this scenario might include knowing if, for example, associates of science in business administration, bachelor of science in health science, certificate in radiologic technology, or certificate in Web design are large or small majors in prior years. If the program is one of the five largest enrollments, then the initial number is likely incorrect. However, the analyst should still search for additional context, such as whether or not the program was recently discontinued at the institution.

Novice institutional researchers may either undervalue context by ignoring it or try to learn about the topic by becoming an expert on their own; neither are a good idea. Experienced institutional researchers know the value of context for the data. As such, they have learned through experiences that there is no substitute for a subject matter expert's (SME) context and thus build relationships with key SMEs. The next sections highlight three areas that institutional researchers can target when developing a relationship with key SMEs.

Data Validation from SMEs.   If we use as an example the above situation regarding the number of political science students, this number could be validated by an institutional employee who works closely with political science students, such as the department chair of the political science department, the dean of the college, or an academic advisor that works directly with political science students. If a relationship was built with any of these individuals, an institutional researcher could make contact to ask for their estimated number to get a ballpark number. Also, if relationships are being built on a regular basis with these individuals, the institutional researcher might recall recent conversations regarding the surge or decline in enrollment in that program.

Improved Understanding of Potential Department-Specific Issues. Building a relationship is not a one-way street. Rather, listening to and understanding department issues and challenges may be helpful to an institutional researcher later on when they are working on a project that involves the topic. For example, academic advising may be implementing a new advising model for some students. When IR connects with the academic advising office asking about any news in the department, hopefully information about the new advising model is shared. The institutional researcher might ask how the new program is going and what successes and challenges they are encountering. This information could prove to be valuable as changes in the data may be seen as a result of the new program, such as changes in enrollment in certain majors.

Essential Intercampus Relationships

No matter if the GE data submission is for one program or all programs at the institution, extracting and reviewing the information take considerable time. In some cases, institutions may be able to leverage premade reports that are integrated into their student information systems. Regardless of how the data are retrieved (i.e., custom query/report or use of a standard report), assistance from multiple departments by their subject-matter expertise for review of the information at the student level and in aggregate is needed. "Because institutional data are often affected by collection mandates and storage issues that are specific to the institution or to a certain area of the institution, it behooves IR professionals to learn as much as possible about the procedures and storage issues at hand" (Kirby & Floyd, 2016). Thus, building relationships with key departments is critical to the successful and accurate reporting of GE data. The next section will describe the most common departments that should be involved with GE reporting, including roles, responsibilities, and skill sets needed from each unit.

In any complex organization, one of the optimum methodologies to maintain relationships is to designate liaisons from the key departments. Many, if not most, higher education institutions qualify as complex organizations. After all, most institutions have a number of independent departments that are driven by the schools' educational mission. Within our institutions, diverse areas of study demand various expertise that, in turn, adds to the cost of providing services, both of which inevitably lead to a more sophisticated organizational configuration. In addition, institutions are made even more complex through historical legacy—"we've always done it this way." And, of course, federal and state regulations add to the complexity of our organizational structures. Each of these departments provide subject-matter or technical experts for their particular area of responsibility, and may even have a slightly different vocabulary if not world view. Although the departments may work together well on a day to day basis with predictable or predetermined tasks, sometimes working outside established channels or procedures can leave gaps in knowledge or communication. Thus, having the proper ad hoc organization for high value projects is essential.

As has been demonstrated above, the GE data request is potentially a high impact event for the institution, and is therefore an ideal situation for implementing a liaison solution for several reasons. First, the data requested for GE are so comprehensive in that they includes key information elements from multiple departments. Second, few institutions will have a single person, or even a single department or office, that will possess sufficient expertise in all the necessary areas to complete the task without outside assistance. Finally, given the high stakes, a distinct disadvantage exists to attempting to complete the GE request in isolation, as the completer will not know what information or required data elements they are missing or misunderstanding. On the contrary, including experts from across the organization will ultimately help mitigate risk to the institution from incomplete and inaccurate reporting of data.

For GE, it is these liaisons that will facilitate, if not provide, necessary information that will assist in extracting, and subsequently validating, the data needed to fulfill the reporting requirements. We have identified six departments that will like be required to provide designated liaisons. However, the number of liaisons will be contingent on the institution's size and organizational structure. For example, some system offices may be pulling the data for multiple institutions and then each institution will need to review and verify their data prior to submission.

Registrar.   The first and arguably one of the most important liaisons is the registrar. Because the registrar's office has the official responsibility for determining who has matriculated, is enrolled, graduated, and withdrew, their role is critical. Appropriate inclusion and exclusion of students hinges upon the registrar's determination of a student's enrollment status. The registrar's data are of particular importance because the students' starting and ending dates for each program are a prerequisite to deriving the financial and financial aid data that are required. If this portion of the data retrieval is inaccurate, all other data will be compromised.

Specifically, the registrar needs to provide a comprehensive list of each student's entry into the institution, subsequent withdrawals and re-entries, and any program changes (such as major or degree level). The goal from a registrar's perspective is to compile a list of the start and end dates a student was active in each program for the entire history of that student. These data will then be used to summarize financial account and financial aid data by program with the use of the start and end dates. For example, take a hypothetical student that entered the institution as a health science major, switched to physical and sport education, then returned to health science. Their tuition charges for their health science program of study would include both enrollment periods in the health science major, but exclude charges associate with their physical and sport education major.

The registrar liaison needs to have an in-depth understanding of entire student life cycle, including enrollment, matriculation, withdrawal, and graduation. This person also needs to understand not only the current policies that are in place, but all significant policy changes that took place during any portion of the reported student's academic career.

Student Financial Aid Office.   The second key area that needs to provide both data and validation is student financial aid (FA). Having a knowledgeable FA liaison is essential to define the required student population and the financial aid data elements in the campus management or financial aid source system. The FA liaison will also be important in validating the results once the data file is complete. The FA liaison needs to have thorough knowledge of a student's financial aid life cycle (awards, disbursements, and refunds) as well as an understanding of the different types of title IV financial aid for their institution (i.e., term or nonterm calendars).

Student Accounts/Finance.   Because the amount of tuition paid is a required GE data element, a third department that will likely need to provide a liaison is student accounts or finance. Having a liaison from finance will help mitigate any confusion as to which types of charges should be included in the GE reporting. Similar to the FA liaison, the finance liaison should be involved in validating the results.

NEW DIRECTIONS FOR INSTITUTIONAL RESEARCH • DOI: 10.1002/ir

The student accounts liaison needs to bring a high awareness of the institution's policy in regards to billing, particularly being able to sort out the different types of charges and credits that can be applied to students' accounts. In addition, this person needs to understand any policy changes that took place that would impact billing, credits, or refunds for any part of the affected student's bill.

Information Technology (IT)/Business Intelligence (BI).   A representative from the intuition's technology department is the fourth likely liaison. Depending on size and organization of the institution, data extraction and reporting may require contacts in the IT or BI department. The BI group could be a subset of IT, or an independent department. Either way, a liaison from the BI or IT department could be critical for data extractions, particularly for large organizations. It is important to understand that not all departments will have sufficient access to their own data. In some cases, the reports they do have may not have adequate data to integrate with data from other departments. For example, the student financial aid office may have inadequate access to the enrollment data from the registrar's office.

The IT or BI liaison needs to have at least a general understanding of where the key data elements lie within the IT systems or data warehouse, and how to obtain appropriate access to those systems. They also need to know what technical tools are available within the organization that can be used compile and export the data to a specified GE format.

Legal/Regulatory Affairs.   The fifth department liaison identified is legal or regulatory affairs. Given the nature of federal reporting and potential impact of GE, obtaining sufficient support from legal or individuals that have expertise in reading and interpreting federal regulations and policies will be helpful and may be required to mitigate the institution's liability. This will include interpretation of regulatory and reporting requirements. At most institutions, legal or regulatory affairs involvement in federal reporting may be rare or nonexistent. However, they may be asked to clarify ambiguous DOE rules or reporting requirements, particularly in the first year of reporting. The legal or regulatory liaison is preferred to have a general understanding of federal reporting requirements and the legal risk to the institution that inaccurate reporting can bring.

Internal Audit.   The final liaison that may be desired is from internal audit. Internal audit groups are frequently found in large organizations to both implement internal controls on key processes and to prepare for external audits. Internal auditors are typically experts in conducting risk assessments, designing internal controls, evaluating compliance with internal procedures and policies, and ensuring conformity to generally accepted industry standards. As such, their role in GE is to ensure that best practices are followed throughout and to mitigate the institution's risk, particularly in case of an outside audit. Because it is best to obtain buy in from internal audits early, having a liaison that can document the GE process from inception to completion will allay concerns and head off difficult questions later. This is particularly true if the internal auditor is part of the development process, and is involved with designing the validation procedures and providing real-time feedback to the rest of the GE group.

Internal audit liaison really just needs to understand their role in the organization, how to document the process thoroughly, and the types of questions that external auditors will want answers to, especially if there are significant negative repercussions to the GE reporting.

Table 6.1 serves as a summary of the key departments and knowledge needed on GE submissions. Additionally, this table can facilitate discussion with the project manager (discussed later in this chapter) and senior leadership by describing the departments involved and the type of knowledge needed so that the appropriate representative is selected.

Table 6.1. Summary of Key Departments and Knowledge

Department	Key Knowledge Needed
Registrar's Office	Understanding of entire student life cycle (enrollment, matriculation, withdrawal, and graduation)
	Current and former policies
Student Financial Aid Office	Financial aid life cycle (awards, disbursements, and refunds)
	Types of title IV financial aid
	Carrying over award years
Student Accounts/Finance	Institution's billing policies
	Past policy changes impacting billing, credits, or refunds
IT/BI	Location of data elements within the IT systems
	Technical tools
Legal/Regulatory Affairs	Federal reporting requirements
	Legal risk to the institution
Internal Audit	Document the process
	Likely external auditor questions

Responsibility and Management

In addition to liaisons to key departments, there are four critical roles that need to be fulfilled: the project manager, business analyst, institutional researcher, and technical lead. Depending on the size of the institution, two or more of these roles may be consolidated into one person. For instance, the institutional researcher might be required to fill the project manager role, or the institutional researcher and technical lead may have to split the business analyst's tasks. However, large institutions will likely favor having each role filled by a different qualified individual because the scope, scale, and complexity of the required work increases with the institution's size. In addition, larger institutions may have individuals with very specialized skill sets that do not translate well into other roles. Finally, splitting the roles among multiple people makes replacing any one individual less impactful, and mitigates the risk to the institution.

NEW DIRECTIONS FOR INSTITUTIONAL RESEARCH • DOI: 10.1002/ir

Project Manager.   Of the four roles, the project manager will be lead person for GE, and will coordinate the work between the business analyst, institutional researcher, technical lead, and the department liaisons (who are the subject-matter experts). The project manager also communicates project challenges and achievements to senior level administrators. It should be the project manager that facilitates setting milestone deadlines and schedules working group meetings to keep the GE project on track. The project manager can either be a senior member of the institution, or a trained or certified project manager. The advantage of having a senior person become the project manager is that they are more likely to have both the connections within the institution and the clout to convey the importance of the GE reporting across the departments. However, with sufficient institutional backing, a certified project management professional (such as a PMP from the Project Management Institute) would also be an excellent choice.

Institutional Researcher.   The second critical role is that of an institutional researcher. The institutional researcher is a key person in the GE reporting process because of his or her unique and specialized knowledge about the institution, its processes, and its data, as well as familiarity with other federal reporting and higher education requirements, standards, and norms. In addition, institutional researchers typically have a background in statistical methods, familiarity with analytical and data reporting tools, strong oral and written communication skills, and assiduous attention to detail. These are all critical skills in assuring the most accurate data are reported to the DOE, giving the institutional researcher an important role to play. Depending on the size of the institution, availability of resources, and technical skill, the institutional researcher may have to fulfill other roles, such as project manager, technical lead, or subject-matter expert.

Business Analyst.   A business analyst is the third critical role that is needed. Although many institutions do not use this title, in this context, the business analyst has an understanding of the institution's processes, systems, and technologies. As such, their role provides adequate documentation of the existing business rules that impact reporting, and documents the technical requirements for GE reporting. This is an individual that could come from the IT, BI, or IR groups, and ideally have experience creating complex requirement documents. Larger organizations will likely prefer to have a dedicated business analyst.

Some may argue that a business analyst is unnecessary, or that creating documentation in addition to the DOE requirements spelled out in the GE User Guide is redundant. However, the DOE GE User Guide does not document any institutional-specific decisions, interpretations of the original DOE requirements, notes as to the origin of the data, equations used to calculate results, or why one field or data point was used over another. Accordingly, the business analysis can translate the DOE requirements through the prism of the institution's business rules into functional requirements and, most importantly, can then translate the reporting functional requirement into technical requirements for the technical lead. In addition, a business analyst can assist the project manager into breaking down the steps into manageable chunks, help set benchmarks, design a rigorous testing protocol, and interface between the subject-matter experts and the technical lead (depending on the technical lead's soft skills).

Technical Lead.   Finally, the technical lead is the individual who will compile or merge the data from the different areas (registrar, financial aid, and finance) with the use of the requirements document provided by the business analyst, and report the data into one of the predefined GE formats. This person will typically be from the IT, BI, or IR groups and have expert technical skill commensurate with the size of the institution and complexity of the data systems. The larger the institution and more complex the institution's data systems, the more technical skill will be required. Because there will be interaction between the technical lead and other departments, such as registrar, financial aid, and finance, it is preferable that the technical lead has good soft skills and be able to communicate technical language into nontechnical terminology. However, technical skills are the most important qualifications for a technical lead and a good business analyst or institutional researcher will be able facilitate the necessary nontechnical communications with other departments.

Table 6.2 outlines the primary roles, tasks, and skills for a GE submission project. Keep in mind that some of the roles may be performed by the same person; however, all roles are needed.

Table 6.2. Summary of Primary Roles, Tasks, and Skills

Role	Tasks	Skills
Project Manager	Schedule and set milestones	Project management
	Communicate with senior leadership	Institutional authority or clout
	Coordinate across institution	
Institutional Researcher	Subject-matter expert	Knowledge of institution, processes, data
	Validate results	
	Augment in areas of concern	Familiarity with federal reporting and higher education requirements
Business Analyst	Documentation of business rules and technical requirements	Knowledge of institution's processes, systems, and technologies
	Coordinate with team and with department liaisons	
Technical Lead	Compile or merge the data from the different areas	Expert technical skill

New Directions for Institutional Research • DOI: 10.1002/ir

Communicating High-Level Results of Data Submitted

Despite existing since 2011, as of the time that this article is being written (late 2015/early 2016) the GE data submission and metrics are still relatively new and have not yet had an opportunity to be thoroughly understood by researchers, policy makers, administrators, and students. Because of the newness of the topic, institutional researchers do not have models, templates, and best practices to refer to when preparing executive summary reports. Therefore, this section aims to identify some of the questions that senior-level leaders may have and possible tables that IR can provide.

Additionally, institutional context is important. Therefore, just as with all reports for senior-level administrators, institutional researchers need to consider current issues for their campus and regular questions that they receive from leaders when preparing the report. In addition to the items listed in Table 6.3, it is important to add appropriately labeled tables (including column labels), sourcing and notes, as well as written interpretation of the information in the tables.

Write bullet statements that point out key items that the reader should see in the tables. Because the preparer of the tables will likely have spent hours with the data, the tables are clear to him or her. However, a senior-level administrator who views information on numerous topics per day will not pick up as quickly on the key points you want him or her to take away without overtly pointing them out.

Table 6.3. Common GE Data Questions and Possible Data IR Can Prepare

#	Senior-Level Administrator Question/Items for the Executive Summary	Possible Information That Institutional Research Can Prepare from the GE Data Set
1	How many records were submitted?	Summary table of records submitted by academic year.
2	Which programs were included/excluded from the submission? Why?	Summary table of records submitted by CIP code and degree level.
3	What financial information was provided?	Summary table of average tuition, books and supplies, and private loan, institutional loans by academic year and status on the last day of the year (i.e., Enrolled = "E," Graduated = "G," and Withdrawn = "W").
4	How is this information similar to IPEDS?	Table showing IPEDS vs. GE numbers on selected items, such as enrollment, graduates, tuition, books and supplies, etc.

NEW DIRECTIONS FOR INSTITUTIONAL RESEARCH • DOI: 10.1002/ir

Implications for Institutional Research Practitioners

This final section discusses three skill areas that IR practitioners who are responsible for GE reporting can enhance to manage GE reporting for their institutions more effectively.

First, institutional researchers should develop skill sets in reading regulations. As the number and complexity of federal requests increase, institutional researchers need to become more comfortable with reading regulatory materials and interpreting them for implications to their institutions. It is important not to rely exclusively on the interpretation of those who are expert in regulations, but not data savvy; otherwise, there can be miscommunication in using wording that can have significant implications. For example, academic year for a financial aid professional refers to the student's financial aid award year (which can vary for each student in continuous enrollment institutions), whereas academic year to an institutional researcher refers to July 1 to June 30, which is used by IPEDS.

Second, institutional researchers should develop project manager skills. Institutional researchers taking a lead role in GE should plan to serve as the coordinator for multiple departments when managing the group to stay on schedule and meet the submission deadline, while juggling unexpected problems. Additionally, the project manager is typically called upon to communicate project updates and challenges to senior-level administrators.

Finally, if a member of the institutional research office is not leading the GE data reporting, institutional researchers should serve as a resource on GE. As GE becomes a greater part of higher education, it is important to identify key resources that institutional stakeholders can refer to for more information. Thus, IR can serve as a repository of such key documents, guides, webinars, etc., that the campus community can use. Additionally, the project manager of the GE reporting may find it useful to create informational materials and presentations for their institution to educate key stakeholders about GE and specific institutional implications. For example, they should provide a list of programs and indicate which institutional programs are and are not subject to the GE regulations and the reasons why.

References

Henderson, A. (2016). Growth of burden in federal and state reporting. *New Directions for Institutional Research, 166*, 23–33. Retrieved from http://onlinelibrary.wiley .com/doi/10.1002/ir.2015.2015.issue-166/issuetoc

Hentschke, G. C., & Parry, S. C. (2014). Innovation in times of regulatory uncertainty: Responses to the threat of "Gainful Employment". *Innovation in Higher Education, 40*, 97–109. Retrieved from http://download.springer.com.proxy1.ncu.edu/static /pdf/458/art%253A10.1007%252Fs10755-014-9298-z.pdf?originUrl=http%3A%2F%

2Flink.springer.com%2Farticle%2F10.1007%2Fs10755-014-9298-z&token2=exp=
1453670160~acl=%2Fstatic%2Fpdf%2F458%2Fart%25253A10.1007%25252

Kirby, Y. K., & Floyd, N. D. (2016). Maximizing institutional research impact through
building relationships and collaborating within the institution. *New Directions for
Institutional Research, 166*, 47–59. Retrieved from http://onlinelibrary.wiley.com/doi
/10.1002/ir.2015.2015.issue-166/issuetoc

National Student Loan Data System. (2015, December 18). *Gainful Employment user
guide.* NSLDS Reference Materials—NSLDS User Documentation. Retrieved from
http://ifap.ed.gov/ifap/byNSLDSType.jsp?type=NSLDS%20User%20Documentation

Serna, G. (2014). The "Gainful Employment rule" and student loan defaults: How the
policy frame overlooks important normative implications. *Journal of Student Financial
Aid, 44*(1). Retrieved from http://publications.nasfaa.org/jsfa

Thompson Coburn. (2014, December 15). *How to project gainful employment rates.*
Retrieved from https://www.thompsoncoburn.com/Libraries/Newsletters/Gainful
_Employment_White_Paper.pdf

U.S. Department of Education. (2014, October 31). Program integrity: Gainful
employment; final rule. Retrieved from http://ifap.ed.gov/fregisters/attachments
/FR103114Final.pdf

U.S. Department of Education. (2015, January). Gainful Employment reporting to
NSLDS webinar. Retrieved from https://www.ifap.ed.gov/presentations/attachments
/2015GEWebinarJan13Jan15.pdf

Xu, A. (2014). Better information for better regulation: How experimentalism can improve the Gainful Employment rule. *Columbia Journal of Law and Social Problems.
48*(1), 57–94.

KRISTINA POWERS *is the associate vice president, Institutional Research Services
at Bridgepoint Education.*

DEREK MACPHERSON *is the data analyst at Bridgepoint Education.*

7

This chapter provides institutional researchers a foundation to understand workforce data and how they can be accessed and used within an institutional research operating culture. Specific wage methodologies, earnings reporting, and future directions for using wage data are provided.

Using State Workforce Data to Examine Postgraduation Outcomes

David R. Troutman, Jessica M. Shedd

The demand for postsecondary outcomes data, in particular data to show a return on investment (ROI) in postsecondary education, is at an all-time high. With tuition and student loan debt continuing to increase, higher education stakeholders and policy makers are placing increased pressure on federal and state governments, institutions, and accreditors to produce this type of information (Rodgers, 2007; Soederberg, 2014; Theline, 2013). At the national level, policymakers have fueled conversations and action through initiatives such as the gainful employment reporting and disclosures, the College Scorecard, and continued debates around the appropriateness of a federal student unit record system.

States across the nation have responded in several ways. Some, such as New York, Wisconsin, and Tennessee, have created laws tying state funding, or portions of state funding, to performance-based metrics that include student earnings and other outcomes-based measures. Florida has performance-based funding for 2-year and 4-year institutions based on job placement, completion rates, retention rates, and first-year median wages for individuals who are employed in Florida 1 year after graduation.

Higher education is a large investment for students, parents, and taxpayers. Among other things, understanding the cost and ROI of attending college empowers students and families to make informed decisions about their education and career. The majority of existing data structures are not designed to produce this type of information, but the landscape is changing quickly and in response, workforce data are being used in conjunction with education data more than ever before.

NEW DIRECTIONS FOR INSTITUTIONAL RESEARCH, no. 169 © 2016 Wiley Periodicals, Inc.
Published online in Wiley Online Library (wileyonlinelibrary.com) • DOI: 10.1002/ir.20172

What Are Workforce Data?

Workforce data—also referred to as labor-market data—are collected for the most part by federal and state agencies. Though data are collected at the individual level, access to that level of data is restricted (The Aspen Institute, 2015). Nonetheless, the aggregate data can be informative for determining labor-market needs and wages, providing benchmarks or context for institution- or program-specific data, and informing students about growth in employment and wages at different education and skill levels.

The most robust examples of workforce data are collected by the U.S. Census Bureau, primarily through the Current Population Survey and the American Communities Survey that allow for state, regional, and national level analyses of educational attainment and earnings based on industry of employment. The Bureau of Labor Statistics (BLS) Occupational Outlook Handbook is perhaps the most well-known of the BLS on-line tools built on labor-market data, and allows users to learn about income, number of current jobs, and projected job growth by occupation. This survey-based data, supplemented by state wage-record data is the basis for the U.S. Census' Longitudinal Employer–Household Dynamics (LEHD) program (The Aspen Institute, 2014 and 2015).

Wage record data are another source of labor-market information. Unlike the U.S. Census and BLS data, wage-record information is not based on surveying individuals, but is instead collected directly from employers. Primary wage-record sources are state UI data systems and federally held tax data. Employer provided tax data (W-2 forms) and the information submitted by the self-employed is maintained by the Internal Revenue Service (IRS) and the Social Security Administration (Zinn and Van Kleunen, 2014). The U.S. Department of Education's Gainful Employment initiative and the recently revamped College Scorecard (2015) both use record-level earnings data from the Social Security Administration.

All of the above data are available to the public in aggregate form, primarily through Web-based tools. Though valuable at the aggregate level, the ability for postsecondary institutions to access individual-level data drastically increases their analytic power and the capacity to answer those questions of outcomes and ROI. For example, record-level workforce data could be linked to educational records, thus producing outcomes data, including pre- and postdegree earnings information, as well as the calculation of informative indicators like a student's postcollegiate debt-to-income ratio. Many states now allow for this type of linkage to occur with their unemployment insurance records, resulting in data that can be analyzed and aggregated to produce new, meaningful, and powerful information at the program, field of study, and institution level.

What Are Unemployment Insurance Wage Data?

Unemployment insurance (UI) is a joint federal-state program. Though there is some flexibility, federal requirements result in general comparability across state UI data systems. On a quarterly basis, employers submit wage-record data—general data on employee's quarterly earnings and employment industry—to the state agency that administers the unemployment insurance program. That agency, typically the state workforce agency, uses the data on an individual's prior work experience to calculate unemployment benefit eligibility (The Aspen Institute, 2014; Zinn and Van Kleunen, 2014). Because these data account for the vast majority of workers in a state over many years, and because it is reported directly by employers, UI wage records are generally considered to be one of the most accurate data sources.

What Unemployment Insurance Data Can and Can't Tell Us

Unemployment insurance wage data provide a wealth of information that has previously not been available to higher education, such as data on which students or graduates are working, in which industry, for how long, and how much they are earning. These data are particularly useful for calculating outcome-based metrics, such as employment rates (the percent of graduates who are employed), as well as how quickly graduates found work after graduation. However, for all the power UI wage records have, there are important limitations to consider.

Out-of-State Employment.   First and foremost, UI data are limited to workers employed in the state. The degree to which this is problematic varies by program, institution, and/or state. Regional institutions or community colleges that primarily serve the local community are less likely to have their students or graduates move out of state; therefore this data limitation may not be particularly problematic. For institutions that attract students from across the country or have graduates that tend to be more mobile postgraduation, UI wage data may represent a smaller percentage of their graduates. Further, there may be particular programs that are more likely to have graduates move out of state, such as business majors relocating to New York or other financial hubs. Most notably, being limited to data for only those employed in-state means that UI wage data does not allow for the calculation of an employment rate of graduates, a sought after number by many. Without data on employment out-of-state, institutions would be underestimating, to varying levels of degree, the true employment rate of graduates. Nonetheless, the data do represent the vast majority of those working in-state, which can be quite informative.

Cross-state collaborations designed to help account for student mobility over state lines could mitigate this data limitation. For example, the Multistate Longitudinal Data Exchange led by the Western Interstate

Commission for Higher Education (WICHE) is a pilot data exchange among four states—Hawaii, Idaho, Oregon, and Washington—that may reveal the feasibility and utility of similar partnerships in the future (WICHE, 2014).

Self-Employment. Another limitation of UI wage data is that self-employment is not included. UI data are reported by employers for the primary purpose of determining unemployment benefits, which are funded by employer-paid unemployment taxes. Because the self-employed do not have an employer reporting on their behalf, they are not included in UI data and do not typically qualify for the unemployment benefit.

Full- or Part-Time Employment. Unemployment insurance wage data are basic information about an individual's employment. In most states, this does not include the number of hours an individual worked or whether or not the individual is considered a full- or part-time employee. Not definitively knowing whether someone is employed full- or part-time is limiting, particularly when studying postgraduate employment. However, proxies can be used to estimate full-time employment, which will be discussed later in this chapter.

Occupation Information. Though not true for all states, the vast majority of unemployment wage databases do not include occupation information. Employers do report the industry of employment using the North American Industry Classification System (NAICS) codes. Though the industry code of the employer is useful information, it does not allow institutions to determine what graduates are doing and whether or not they are employed in their field of study. Job placement rates—specifically an "in-field" rate—has received a lot of attention, particularly with respect to gainful employment disclosure requirements and, in some cases, program-specific reporting requirements for accreditors and state agencies.

For example, an individual may be employed in the retail trade industry working for a grocery store chain, but it is not known whether the individual works as a cashier, a buyer, a human resources professional, an accountant or fiscal officer, a pharmacist, or any number of other occupations involved in operating a grocery store. Occupations or jobs in any of the industries vary widely and a graduate could be working in-field in almost any industry.

Alaska is an example of a state that already collects occupation information through their UI wage system. Other states are working to follow suit. For example, the Louisiana Workforce Commission recently announced changes to their reporting: effective January 2016, the employee's occupational code or job title, as well as the hourly rate of pay, will also be required.

Location of Employment. Lastly, though some states' UI wage data do include the location of the employer, this location does not always equate to where the employee actually works and lives. In some cases, employer location is the same thing as where the employee works, but in other cases, the employer location may be the location of the central payroll office, for example. This ambiguity makes it difficult to assess the extent that

NEW DIRECTIONS FOR INSTITUTIONAL RESEARCH • DOI: 10.1002/ir

wages vary within a state or to evaluate the mobility of graduates within the state.

Despite these limitations, state unemployment insurance wage data have allowed for some institutions, systems, and states to answer important questions of postgraduation outcomes and ROI with confidence and reliability. As a result, the demand for access to UI wage data has drastically increased.

Data Access, Data-Sharing Agreements, and Data Security

Availability of UI data varies considerably by state. Similar to how states have some flexibility with the structure of their UI wage data system, each state has authority to set the terms under which that data are made available. Further, limited state agency resources to respond to data requests, and in some cases individual or state interpretation of FERPA restrictions, also contribute to the difference in data availability across states (The Aspen Institute, 2014 and 2015).

In states where the data have been made available, postsecondary institutions may be able to request data about their students or graduates from the appropriate state agency. To ensure confidentiality, data are only returned to the requesting institution in aggregate, as averages or medians, suppressing data when the number of cases is determined to be too small. Institutions can provide social security numbers for a particular graduating cohort, or graduating cohorts across several years, in a particular degree program, for example. The state agency can then match the social security numbers with the available UI wage records and return aggregate data on the number of those graduates found to be employed in-state, their average and median quarterly or annual earnings, and in some cases their industries of employment, while maintaining individual confidentiality (The Aspen Institute, 2014).

In other states, after establishing data-sharing agreements that specify the required data protection and security protocols, data have been made available to institutions and higher education systems at the individual level. This, of course, allows for the most robust analysis of pre- and postcollegiate work among the many other analyses that can be conducted once the UI data are linked to education records. Several of these analyses will be discussed later in the chapter. Institutions interested in determining if a particular state has a current data-sharing agreement should contact the Department of Labor within their state. If no agreement exists, there are several resources designed to assess the current state of linking workforce data with educational data in the different states produced both by State Higher Education Executive Officers and the Workforce Data Quality Campaign. In addition, the U.S. Department of State's Collaboratory and the nonprofits The Aspen Institute (2014) and FHI 360 have resources that assist users in developing data-sharing agreements. These resources are excellent guides for those looking to develop their first data-sharing agreements of this kind. The process can be a very time-consuming effort; however, the benefits of accessing these data outweigh the costs.

Typical Variables in a UI Wage Data Set

The variables in the UI data set depend on the terms of the data-sharing agreement with the state agency responsible for the UI data. UI wage data are reported by year and quarter (e.g., 20051, 20052, 20053, and 20054). Typically, the variables include company name, location of company, federal employer identification number (FEIN), North American Industry Classification System (NAICS) code, and wage information for the employee.

Some of these variables, like company name, address, and FEIN have limited analytical use. Often, institutions are prohibited from using or reporting company name, and the limitations of the location data were discussed above. Even though these variables are not as useful for analysis, they can be useful when validating and cleaning data.

Although industry is not the same as occupation, the NAICS code is still a valuable analytic and reporting variable. It is a six-digit number that classifies businesses into various industry classifications, or economic activity types. The first two digits of the NAICS code represent the business sector (e.g., 23: Construction; 61: Educational Services; and 62: Health Care and Social Services). The third digit represents the subsector (e.g., 622: Hospitals and 623: Nursing and Residential Care Facilities). The fourth digit represents the industry group (e.g., 6221: General Medical Surgical Hospitals and 6231: Nursing Care Facilities). The fifth digit represents the NAICS industries, and the sixth digit represents the national industries. There are a total of 1,170 industries that are identified in the NAICS codes (http://www.census.gov/eos/www/naics/).

If permitted by the data-sharing agreement, the data set may also include the agreed-upon student identifier, allowing the workforce data to be linked to the student record data.

Structure of the Data. A UI wage data set has very few variables (typically around 20 columns). However, the hierarchical structure of the data is where it becomes complex. There is typically one record per person, per employer, and per quarter. The lowest level of the unit of analysis is the number of employers for students per quarter.

Depending on the state, the wage record might be limited by the number of characters in the field. For example, the Texas Workforce Commission limits the number of characters in wage field to five. Within the Texas wage data set, the record can range from zero dollars to 99,999 dollars. If the wage exceeds this maximum amount, then an additional case (row) will be added to the same year and quarter with the remaining wages earned by the graduate.

Because of this complexity, an institution's student data set might include 100,000 students, but the resulting workforce data set might include millions of cases (rows), as seen in Table 7.1.

Table 7.1. Example of an Institution's Student Data Set, Which Might Include 100,000 Students, but the Resulting Workforce Data Set Might Include Millions

Person ID	YR+Q	Employer	Wage
SID001	20151	EmployerA	Wage1
SID001	20151	EmployerB	Wage1 (greater than 99,999)
SID001	20151	EmployerB	Wage2
SID001	20152	EmployerB	Wage1
SID002	20152	EmployerA	Wage1

Data Cleaning and Preparation for Analysis.   The goal in cleaning and preparing data for analysis is to reduce the systematic error that will impact the validity of a UI wage sample. The majority of the time spent working with UI wage data sets will be reviewing, cleaning, and constructing new variables. It is important to save the original returned data file and then use a working data file when cleaning and modifying the data. The data set may contain several types of errors (outlined below), but there are steps that can be taken to ensure that the data are accurate and reliable.

The cleaning process is investigative work that can be overwhelming at times. Using a decision tree, Figure 7.1 can assist in the data cleaning by bifurcating the sample into cases with error and without error. First, determine the cases that do have reliable and valid information, based on the individual's name, within a given quarter and over time. Then focus on the cases that are inconsistent and have errors. Errors might include invalid social security numbers (SSN), multiple names tied to the same SSN, and duplicate records reported. When this happens, a decision needs to be made to determine what cases will be kept in the data set, and what cases will be censored.

Invalid social security numbers.   Some student social security numbers may turn out to be invalid. It is important to make sure the social security numbers in the data set are clean. Most of this cleaning should happen on the institution's student data set before the institution submits its file to the agency for matching. Any social security number with all zeros in a digit group (e.g., 000-XX-XXXX, XXX-00-XXXX, and XXX-XX-0000) should be filtered out before submission. Sometimes invalid SSNs result from student IDs assigned to foreign students. These invalid SSNs (e.g., 123456789, 111111111, 012345678, and 001234567) should also be removed before submission. Invalid SSNs may also occur if the SSNs were incorrectly entered into the student information system. These errors may not become apparent until after the data set is matched and returned.

Figure 7.1. Example Decision Tree for Data-Cleaning Process

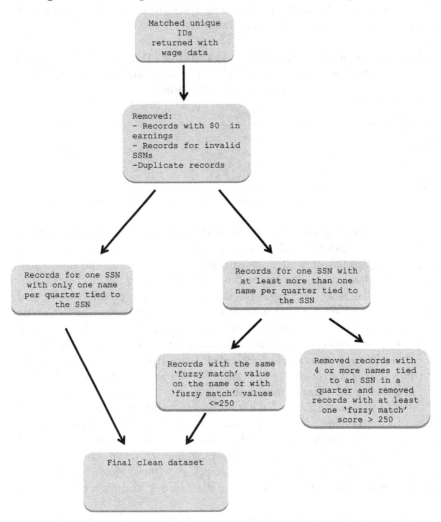

Multiple names associated with the same SSN.   Another error that may be found in the data is a single SSN that is tied to multiple people. For example, within the UI wage data set, John Smith and Anne Jones have the same SSN and have wages reported for the same year and quarter. It can be difficult to determine if it is the same person or not. A case might be someone who changed his or her name (typically last name) or had their name modified by their employer when submitting the workforce data to the state. There may also be cases where the SSN is clearly shared by different individuals. It is vital that the right person be tied to the right wage. The best approach for this SSN error is to create a filter variable, flag these cases, systematically examine each of them, and then establish logic on which cases might need to be censored in the data.

Duplicate records.   Another error that may be found in the data is duplicate records of the same person within the same quarter with identical employment and earnings information. If this occurs and is not corrected, it will inflate the overall annual earnings for the student as well as possibly increase the median annual earnings for the population.

Determining the Unit of Analysis.   UI wage data are usually structured where the unit of analysis is a wage record per employer within a given year and quarter. The UI wage data contain multiple layers of nested data because students can have multiple employers within a single year and quarter. The layers can become complex depending on how long the student resides in the state and the number of jobs the student has over time.

It is important to determine the unit of analysis prior to conducting any type of analyses. In the data set's original format, the data are prepared for analysis to examine employer information and industries students are working in during a given time period. To explore how much students make in a given year or how student characteristics might impact earnings, however, the data set needs to be modified. Wage records would need to be summed by quarter and then summed by calendar year in order to calculate wage information. This flattens the data, so that each student is one case/row. Once the data are cleaned and restructured, the match rates of the student population can be calculated.

Consider Representativeness of Sample Found in UI Wage Data

Limitations in who is captured in the UI wage data and cases that are censored during the data cleansing will impact the percentage of students represented in the UI wage data—the match rate. This rate can inform discussions of relevancy and accuracy and answer questions about whether the UI wage sample is a true representation of the student population. For this reason, it is important to remain transparent and always indicate match rates when reporting student earnings.

Match Rates.   Calculating a series of match rates will determine whether UI wage samples are representative of the population. Rates should be calculated at the institution, degree, program, and student levels. Because the data contain wage records over time, the match rates should also be reported from year to year. Figure 7.2 provides an example of the number of cohorts and years of earnings represented in a UI wage data set. Examining match rates for each cohort for each year can provide insightful information on how earnings records might vary by cohort and over time.

An overall match rate for the institution would represent the number of total students found within the UI wage data divided by the number of total valid SSNs that were submitted to the state workforce agency. The number of valid SSNs is determined during the data-cleaning process. It

Figure 7.2. Earnings by Cohort Year

		Earnings by Year									
		1st	2nd	3rd	4th	5th	6th	7th	8th	9th	10th
Cohort Year	2002	✓	✓	✓	✓	✓	✓	✓	✓	✓	✓
	2003	✓	✓	✓	✓	✓	✓	✓	✓	✓	✓
	2004	✓	✓	✓	✓	✓	✓	✓	✓	✓	
	2005	✓	✓	✓	✓	✓	✓	✓	✓		
	2006	✓	✓	✓	✓	✓	✓	✓			
	2007	✓	✓	✓	✓	✓	✓				
	2008	✓	✓	✓	✓	✓					
	2009	✓	✓	✓	✓						
	2010	✓	✓	✓							
	2011	✓	✓								
	2012	✓									

is recommended that match rates are produced for at least the following categories: degree level (certificates, associate's, bachelor's, master's, PhD, and professional), gender; race/ethnicity, and residency status at the time of admission (state resident, out-of-state resident, and foreign).

Probability of Not Being Found in UI Wage Data. Using predictive modeling (logistic regression) is another strategy to determine whether a sample is representative of the population. Logistic regression can be used to model the data where the independent variables (gender, race/ethnicity, state residency, and degree level) are used to predict a dichotomous dependent variable (wage record found/wage record not found). The logistic regression analyses will indicate if the independent variables are statistically significant in predicting the outcome. For example, out-of-state residents might be more likely to be missing in the wage records compared to in-state residents. This data analytic approach can be very helpful. Please refer to Pampel's (2000) paper entitled "Logistic regression: A primer for a further explanation of logistic regression."

National Student Clearinghouse. Some students who receive a degree continue on to receive additional education. These students may or may not be working. Moreover, these students might have moved outside the state to attend school. The National Student Clearinghouse Student Tracker consists of past and current student enrollment information from higher education institutions within the United States. Student Tracker accounts for more than 3,600 colleges and universities (98% of the students enrolled in private and public U.S. institutions). Data from Student Tracker can assist in increasing overall match rates by providing valuable information about where students go after graduating. Submitting the name and birth date based on the valid SSNs to Student Tracker

NEW DIRECTIONS FOR INSTITUTIONAL RESEARCH • DOI: 10.1002/ir

might provide additional information on students not found in the UI wage data set. For more information on Student Tracker, please refer to http://www.studentclearinghouse.org/colleges/studenttracker/.

An example of match rates by current status of student population can be found in Figure 7.3. The pie chart indicates students' work status and enrollment status. Seventy-eight percent of students were found in the UI wage records 1 year after graduating, which means they were found working in the state. Of those, 17% were also found in the Student Tracker, meaning that they were working and enrolled in school. An additional 6% of students were found by Student Tracker to be enrolled in a college or university outside the state.

Figure 7.3. Match Rates by Current Status of Student

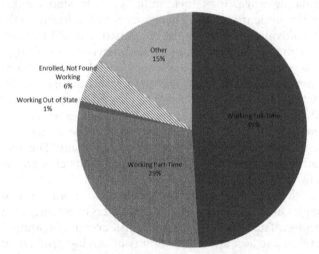

In this example, 1% of the student population was found working out of state by using the Wage Record Interchange System 2 (WRIS 2) data repository. WRIS 2 is a wage data agreement among 39 states (it excludes some more populous states like California, Colorado, New York, and Georgia). Institutions must establish a contractual agreement in order to match any student record data to the repository. After the matching occurs, an aggregate report will be sent to the institution indicating the total of students found in the repository. For more information on WRIS 2, please refer to the U.S. Department of Labor.

Fifteen percent of students were not found in the data sources for the search (represented as "Other" in Figure 7.3). These students might work out of state, in California, New York, or other states not participating in WRIS 2; they may have left the country, be self-employed, unemployed, might have never entered the workforce, or may be deceased. Overall, the pie chart indicates that 85% of the student population was accounted for 1 year after graduating.

Methodology for Determining Postgraduate Earnings

Choosing a methodology when determining how to calculate postgraduate earnings is by far the most important decision that needs to be made when working with UI wage data. To date, there is no agreed-upon methodology to calculate postgraduate earnings. When calculating annual wages, there are a number of decision points to consider: the time period when earnings should be accounted for postgraduation, deciding whether or not to use one quarter versus four quarters of earnings, determining a proxy for full-time employment, and deciding how to handle when a student received multiple degrees. The next section will provide some guidance on how to calculate annual earnings, including how best to adjust for inflation.

Calculating Annual Wage.   There are several things to consider when calculating wage. First, determine when to start capturing wage records for the student cohorts. There are several different methodologies that are currently used. For example, the Department of Education's Scorecard uses an *entering* cohort approach and determines earnings for individuals at 10 years after entering the school for individuals who receive any federal financial aid. Others working with wage records use an *exiting* cohort approach when calculating earnings (Maguire, Starobin, Santos Laanan, & Friedel, 2012; Sanchez & Santos Laanan, 1997; Schneider, 2015). The timing is based on waiting two to three quarters after the student's graduation from an institution before calculating wage for students. This two-to-three quarter waiting period provides the degree recipients enough time to find employment.

Second, determine the number of quarters to use when calculating annual earnings. One approach is to use four quarters of earnings data to create annual earnings. This approach provides a true account for annual earnings because it takes into account the continuity of employment over the length of a year. Another approach is to use one quarter of wage records to provide a proxy for annual earnings. Because this approach only requires matching to one quarter instead of a full four quarters, it will increase the match rates.

The majority of the UI wage data that state agencies collect from employers does not provide the number of hours worked, so no indicators for full-time and part-time status are provided. Therefore, a proxy for "full-time" status could be created from the data. One approach is to define full-time as individuals who are working in all four quarters within a calendar year and have quarterly earnings of greater than or equal to $3,298.75 for all of those four quarters. To arrive at that figure, 35 hours in a work week is multiplied by the federal minimum wage ($7.25 per hour) and then multiplied by the 13 weeks in a quarter (35 hours $\times$ $7.25 $\times$ 13 weeks = $3,298.75).

Postgraduate Earnings Reporting.   As workforce data become more accessible, different examples of how to "report" or display information on students' earnings after graduation are surfacing. The U.S. Department of Education in 2015 updated the College Scorecard to include students' postgraduation earnings. This interactive on-line tool empowers students to choose a college based on data on a number of other factors, such as cost of attendance, retention and graduation rates, financial aid and debt, academic programs, and location of the institution. The tool provides median salary at the institution level compared to the national average. However, given the limitations of unit record data held by the Department, the salary information is based only on students who received federal financial aid. Further, it is captured only at 10 years after a student enters the institution. Although including this salary information on the Scorecard is a good start, there are limitations to reporting earnings at the institutional level, as well as reporting only for a censored group (those who receive federal financial aid). Reporting earnings of the broader student population, by degree major, provides a more accurate and realistic outlook that accounts for program differences (e.g., STEM vs. non-STEM).

Given the value of knowing the earnings by degree for graduates, higher education systems and campuses are discovering creative and beneficial ways to showcase this information, including using wage records to create dashboards and interactive reports to inform stakeholders.

Dashboards and Interactive Reports.   Creating dashboards and interactive reports can be very informative for students and their families, university administration, state legislators, and general public. It is opportunity for higher education institutions to take a lead in this effort. There are several higher education systems, universities, and organizations that are making headway on the postcollegiate outcomes efforts. Three examples of these efforts are from College Measures, California Community Colleges, and The University of Texas System.

College Measures.   College Measures (www.collegemeasures.org) is a multistate effort to create a dashboard that allows students and parents to explore median first-year earnings, average time to degree, and average tuition and fees by program and by institution. Arkansas, Colorado, Florida, Tennessee, Texas, and Virginia are currently participating in this effort.

California Community Colleges.   The California Community Colleges Chancellor's office developed an interactive, on-line tool called Salary Surfer. Salary Surfer (http://salarysurfer.cccco.edu/SalarySurfer.aspx) provides information to students and parents on earnings of recent graduates who received a certificate or associates degree from specific disciplines from California Community Colleges. It provides median salaries 2 years prior to receiving a certificate or associates degree, and 2 or 5 years after receiving the award.

The University of Texas System.   The University of Texas System has created an interactive, on-line tool called seekUT (search+earnings+ employment=knowledge, www.utsystem.edu/seekut). The purpose in creating the Web site and tool is to use real earnings of real graduates to help current and perspective students set realistic expectations for college and career planning. Moreover, the Web site and tool provide the earnings data within the context of additional information, such as student debt, degree requirements, and job growth.

UT System worked with students from its many institutions to create an on-line tool that provide students with information by degree major on postcollegiate median earnings (1, 5, and 10 years after graduation), average loan debt, estimated monthly loan payment, debt-to-income ratios, degree credit requirements, time to degree, the percentage of students who continue their education within 1 year after graduating, and the types of industries recent UT System graduates are working in. The tool uses data from the U.S. Department of Labor's Bureau of Labor Statistics, and also provides job projections and median earnings for occupations among the 50 states.

Future Directions for Using Wage Data

The majority of colleges and universities do not have access to student-level wage records in order to produce reports and dashboards on postcollegiate outcomes. Others may only be able to access data in aggregate form, which is more limiting from an analytic perspective, but still provides more insight into postcollegiate outcomes than higher education has generally had before. As stated earlier, each state establishes its own policies regarding the terms under which the UI data are made available. For those systems, state agencies for higher education, and individual institutions interested in working towards obtaining UI wage data in their state, they can work to develop relationships and agreements with their state workforce agencies (Department of Labor, Workforce Commission, etc.) to allow for such collaborations. In fact, they can use examples of existing successful collaborations and resulting research and tools to help start the conversation about how the data would be used and the purpose behind higher education being interested in accessing UI wage data sources. Alternatively, for those states with state longitudinal data systems, there may be opportunities to conduct specific research projects utilizing the data. Ideas for future research are discussed below that could advance research and perhaps help guide conversations with state workforce agencies and stewards of longitudinal data systems.

Colleges and universities that do have access to student-level wage records are beginning to think about future research, beyond descriptive statistics to examine the correlations associated with student earnings. For example, research is needed to examine the relationship among gender, race/ethnicity, degree program (STEM vs. non-STEM), and student earnings.

The University of Texas System is conducting this type of work. With over 10 years of earnings data for undergraduates who attended a University of Texas System institution, quantile regression, and factorial ANOVA analyses are used to analyze differences in earnings between those completing their degree and those who left without earning their degree. This is one way to begin to show the value of a degree. In addition, the differences in earnings across student demographics including gender and race/ethnicity show wage gap patterns similar to those nationally. Further, these gaps persist even among bachelor's degree earners in STEM fields. This type of analysis can be informative to policymakers at all levels, students (particularly as they negotiate salaries in their first jobs), as well as career offices and student affairs professionals at colleges and universities as they consider preparing students with future earnings expectations as well as interview and salary negotiation skills.

Although how colleges and universities may be able to access wage data in the future is unknown (via state UI wage records, state longitudinal data systems, or even a federal unit record system), much can be done to expand current capabilities and research, for example, more collaboration among colleges and universities to answer research questions across state lines. The City University of New York System, University of Texas System, and State University System of Florida are currently working together to answer the following types of questions:

- Are there certain types of students who are more likely to be missing from earnings data?
- Do students' median annual salaries vary based on the sampling strategy chosen by institutional researchers? Do annual earnings differ when comparing completers, noncompleters, and all students?
- Does the number of STEM degrees offered at an institution inflate the institutional annual earnings reported?

This collaboration will assist in moving the needle on understanding the strengths and weaknesses of using UI wage data and the ability for states to work together utilizing wage data.

References

The Aspen Institute (2014). *Using Labor Market Data to Improve Student Success.* Retrieved from http://www.aspeninstitute.org/sites/default/files/content/docs/pubs /LaborMarketDataGuide.pdf

The Aspen Institute, College Excellence Program (2015). *From college to jobs: Making sense of labor market returns to higher education.* Retrieved from http://www .aspeninstitute.org/sites/default/files/content/docs/pubs/LaborMarketReturns_0.pdf

Maguire, K. J., Starobin, S. S., Santos Laanan, F., & Friedel, J. N. (2012). Measuring the accountability of CTE Programs: Factors that influence postcollege earnings among community college students. *Career and Technical Education Research, 37*(3), 235–261.

Pampel, F. C. (2000). *Logistic regression: A primer.* Thousand Oaks, CA: Sage.

Rodgers, T. (2007). Measuring value added in higher education: A proposed methodology for developing a performance indicator based on the economic value added to graduates. *Education Economics, 15*(1), 55–74.

Sanchez, J. R., & Santos Laanan, F. (1997). The economic returns of a community college education. *Community College Review, 25*(3), 73–87.

Schneider, M. (2015). *Education pays in Colorado: Earnings 1, 5, and 10 years after college.* Report produced for the College Measures' Economic Success Project.

Soederberg, S. (2014). Student loans, debtfare and the commodification of debt: The politics of securitization and the displacement of risk. *Critical Sociology, 40*(5), 687–709.

Theline, J. R. (2013). *The rising costs of higher education: A reference handbook.* Santa Barbara, CA: ABC-CLIO, LLC.

WICHE. (2014, December). *Building capacity for tracking human capital development and its mobility across state lines (WICHE Policy Insights brief).* Boulder, CO: WICHE.

Zinn, R., & Van Kleunen, A. (2014, January). *Making workforce data work.* Workforce Data Quality Campaign. Retrieved from http://www.workforcedqc.org/sites /default/files/Resource%20PDF/WDQC%20report.pdf

Appendix

Resources: Data Access and Sharing Agreements.   Chinoy, M. R. (April 2016). Making the Most of Workforce Data: State Collaboration with External Entities for Actionable Research. Workforce Data Quality Campaign. http://www.workforcedqc.org/sites/default/files/images/WDQC-MakingtheMostofWorkforceData-web.pdf

The Aspen Institute (2014). Using labor market data to improve student success. http://www.aspeninstitute.org/sites/default/files/content/docs/ pubs/LaborMarketDataGuide.pdf

Feldbaum, M., & Harmon, T. (2012). Using unemployment insurance wage data to improve program employment outcomes: A technical assistance guide for community and technical colleges. The Collaboratory and FHI360. file:///C:/Users/jshedd/Downloads/Using%20UI%20Wage%20Data .pdf

Garcia, T. I., & L'Orange H. P. (2012, November). *Strong foundations: The state of postsecondary data systems.* Boulder, CO: SHEEO. http://www .sheeo.org/sites/default/files/publications/20130107%20StrongFoundations Update_Finalc.pdf

U.S. Department of Education, National Center for Education Statistics: Privacy Technical Assistance Center (PTAC): https://nces.ed.gov /programs/ptac/Home.aspx State Longitudinal Data Systems (SLDS) Grant Program resources: https://nces.ed.gov/programs/slds/

DAVID R. TROUTMAN *is the associate vice chancellor for institutional research and decision support at The University of Texas System.*

JESSICA M. SHEDD *is the assistant director for institutional research and reporting at The University of Texas System.*

INDEX

NEW DIRECTIONS FOR INSTITUTIONAL RESEARCH

ORDER FORM SUBSCRIPTION AND SINGLE ISSUES

DISCOUNTED BACK ISSUES:

Use this form to receive 20% off all back issues of *New Directions for Institutional Research*.
All single issues priced at **$23.20** (normally $29.00)

TITLE   ISSUE NO.   ISBN

_____   _____   _____
_____   _____   _____
_____   _____   _____

*Call 1-800-835-6770 or see mailing instructions below. When calling, mention the promotional code JBNND to receive
your discount. For a complete list of issues, please visit www.wiley.com/WileyCDA/WileyTitle/productCd-IR.html*

SUBSCRIPTIONS: (1 YEAR, 4 ISSUES)

☐ New Order   ☐ Renewal

     U.S.   ☐ Individual: $89   ☐ Institutional: $362
     CANADA/MEXICO   ☐ Individual: $89   ☐ Institutional: $404
     ALL OTHERS   ☐ Individual: $113   ☐ Institutional: $440

Call 1-800-835-6770 or see mailing and pricing instructions below.
Online subscriptions are available at www.onlinelibrary.wiley.com

ORDER TOTALS:

     Issue / Subscription Amount: $ _____

           Shipping Amount: $ _____
(for single issues only – subscription prices include shipping)
            Total Amount: $ _____

SHIPPING CHARGES:	
First Item	$6.00
Each Add'l Item	$2.00

*(No sales tax for U.S. subscriptions. Canadian residents, add GST for subscription orders. Individual rate subscriptions must
be paid by personal check or credit card. Individual rate subscriptions may not be resold as library copies.)*

BILLING & SHIPPING INFORMATION:

☐ **PAYMENT ENCLOSED:** *(U.S. check or money order only. All payments must be in U.S. dollars.)*

☐ **CREDIT CARD:**   ☐ VISA   ☐ MC   ☐ AMEX

     Card number _____Exp. Date_____

     Card Holder Name_____Card Issue # _____

     Signature _____Day Phone_____

☐ **BILL ME:** *(U.S. institutional orders only. Purchase order required.)*

     Purchase order # _____
                 Federal Tax ID 13559302 • GST 89102-8052

Name_____

Address_____

Phone_____ E-mail_____

Copy or detach page and send to: **John Wiley & Sons, Inc. / Jossey Bass**
                                 PO Box 55381
                                 Boston, MA 02205-9850

PROMO JBNND